Preventing
Preparing
Pursuing

A Self-Help Guide to Resolving Disputes Headed for Small Claims Court

Cary Rosenthal

Preventing Preparing Pursuing
Cary Rosenthal
Preventing, Preparing, Pursuing, L.L.C.

ISBN 978-0-9899093-0-3
Library of Congress Control Number: 2013915705

Printed in the United States of America by BookLogix

Forth Printing August 2016

For information about ordering, please contact Cary Rosenthal at cr21740@aol.com

About the Author

Cary Rosenthal is a registered civil mediator with the Georgia Office of Dispute Resolution. As a member of the mediation staff for the Magistrate Court of Cobb County, Georgia, he has conducted more than 1,500 mediation conferences. Additionally, Rosenthal has served the State Bar of Georgia as a non-attorney fee arbitrator and has heard more than 250 cases.

A retired printing, publishing and advertising entrepreneur, Rosenthal has been a party to numerous contracts ranging from corporate acquisitions, purchases and sales of commercial and residential real estate, employment contracts as an employer, employee, and compensation committee chair for a public company, issues dealing with intellectual property, and contracts for the purchases and sales of goods and services.

Among his leadership positions for the Printing and Imaging Association of Georgia, Cary chaired the legal committee, which served as a liaison with the attorneys retained by the organization. He later served the PIAG as Chairman of the Board.

During the formative years of his synagogue, he drafted its first formal set of by-laws and later served as President.

Over the entire twenty-year span of ownership, his companies had never been sued. The minimal amounts of lawsuits filed by his companies were mainly in pursuit of non-payment for services rendered.

Acknowledgements

Most book authors will acknowledge that it takes a "village" of people working with them to produce the end results. My preferred term for those who helped me is "enablers," without whom this book would have been impossible for me to accomplish.

Recognition must first go to George Fox, my long-time attorney and friend who recommended me to the State Bar of Georgia as a non-attorney arbitrator for its Fee Arbitration program. Thanks also to Program Manager, Rita Payne, who continues to call me to hear cases some three decades later.

Among those most instrumental in steering me toward a successful mediation career is another long-time friend and mentor, Alan Granath, who began his second career as a mediator ten years earlier than I. The combination of his intriguing case histories over the years and the offer to be my advisor convinced me to sign up for mediation training.

Alan was also right on target with his recommendation that I train at the Justice Center of Atlanta. Edie Primm, the Center's Director and former Board Chairperson of the Georgia Office of Dispute Resolution, did a superb job training my class. What I learned at the JCA gave me an excellent foundation for what was to come.

Significant among those who enabled me was Herb Wollner, a friend and former community service colleague, and a member of the mediation team for the Magistrate Court of Cobb County. It was his personal introduction of me to Tracie Grabarkewitz, Judicial Program Coordinator that contributed to my appointment.

Tracie, more than any other person, was responsible for giving me my first opportunity to mediate professionally, resulting in my being in a position to seriously contemplate writing this book. She has been a teacher, mentor, excellent manager, and most importantly, provided a model for the treatment of those seeking to resolve disputes.

In addition to the research necessary to write this book, much of what has been documented is based on personal experiences. To review my perspective and offer suggestions, I

iv

asked my courthouse colleagues; Judge Timothy Wolfe and mediators Lorraine Cruse and Herb Wollner who gladly did so. They also served as test readers, as did Alan Granath and George Fox. Their assistance was invaluable.

I also called upon Judges Jennifer Inmon, Luke Mayes, and Philip Taylor who always exercised great patience and shared their knowledge in answering my endless questions.

The final step prior to production was the editing. The initial phase was masterfully handled by Ruby Burgis. The last eyes to review the manuscript were those of one of my oldest and closest friends, Ron Ruthfield. Ron is not only a fine novelist in his own right, but is an astute marketing professional, who also helped me to navigate the new, fast-changing world of digital publishing and distribution.

Finally, my deepest appreciation goes to my talented daughter, Kimberly Myerson, who learned the art of typography and design while observing in the creative department of my Atlanta-based company, Phoenix Communications. A daughter helping her dad often requires significant composure when designing and formatting a book. Luckily, Kimberly has an abundance of equanimity; perhaps a bit more than her father.

Contents

Preparing

Pursuing

Foreword

The writing of "Preventing, Preparing, Pursuing..." was motivated by my ongoing observations in the courtroom and mediation conference rooms of disputing parties who may have been able to resolve a dispute prior to going to court. In addition, I have determined they probably could have been much better prepared when they had their day in court.

For sure, this is not a textbook, but an easy-to-read how-to guide intended to aid the average person who may be unfamiliar with ways to handle disputes that could eventually lead to a lawsuit in small claims court. As you read, you will encounter the use of commonly used legal terms, but they will always be defined in plain language.

I am sure many of you have at one time or another tried to help settle differences with family members, co-workers, neighbors, and friends. In many ways you were, without realizing it, playing the role of a mediator. Over the years, warring parties frequently seemed to find their way to my doorstep, too. My efforts to resolve their disputes, combined with my affection for law-oriented TV shows and legal thrillers, seems to have set a course for me to become involved in mediation on a formal basis, as well as writing a book of this nature.

My first professional exposure to conflict resolution began in the early 1980s when I became a Fee Arbitrator for the State Bar of Georgia. This firsthand experience taught me the nuances of a legal hearing from the inside. After assisting with countless fee arbitration cases, my formal training in mediation seemed to be a natural progression, which culminated in my appointment to the mediation staff of the Cobb County Georgia Magistrate Court.

More than fifteen hundred cases later, I find myself excited by the possibility of helping a wide variety of people via this guide. In outlining the book, it seemed logical to present dispute resolution in three phases: 1) **Preventing** conflicts; 2) **Preparing** someone to be ready for court either as a plaintiff or defendant; 3) **Pursuing** and collecting a monetary award.

In most cases, as I listen to parties make their opening statements, I can't help but think that they could have avoided their conflicts by using common sense, less emotion and a little cooperation.

The first section of the book, **Preventing**, deals with conflict prior to a lawsuit being filed by offering suggestions for mutually successful contract negotiation when purchasing or providing a product or service. But remember, once the parties are in court, it is too late for prevention.

It also offers information regarding communications between the parties, both pre- and post- contract, and takes particular note when conflicts begin to occur. It also covers how to make a last ditch effort to settle a dispute before a lawsuit is filed.

The **Preparing** section covers information on hiring an attorney; filing a lawsuit; organizing evidence; knowing what to expect in a court room; understanding the option of mediation; and comprehending the resulting documentation from a mediated settlement or a court ruling. For many people, going to court is a new experience. Plaintiffs and defendants are often nervous, might not understand the procedures and may not be properly prepared. Therefore, close examination and study of this book's second section should make both sides feel more comfortable with the judicial or mediation process.

The third portion of the book provides cogent information on **Pursuing** the outcome of a settled dispute. Whether a hearing is heard in court or an agreement is reached in mediation, there are obligations that follow the outcome. The prevailing party is often concerned about the losing party living up to his or her obligations, including the collecting of a monetary judgment. Other matters concern the adherence by either party to a mediated settlement. A brief discussion regarding appeals of cases, sometimes considered by the losing party (or less frequently, the winning party,) is also included, along with the obvious nuances associated with taking further action.

Please do not take anything in this book, written or implied, to be legal advice. Further, do not rely on anything in this book as a reason to do or not do something. To answer

any questions inspired by what you will be reading, consult with an attorney or search the Internet for more basic information. You may also wish to contact Clark Howard, a popular radio talk show host syndicated in more than 200 stations across the U.S. As a media personality and consumer advocate, his on-air advice has undoubtedly helped innumerable people avoid legal entanglements. Check online for when Howard's show airs in your area.

It is important to note that the information in this book pertains only to small claims court, where most parties go without having to hire legal representation. Also, all courts at this level allow lawsuits to be heard within a maximum dollar amount, which varies from state to state.

Mostly, the small claims courts in Georgia are my points of reference. You are encouraged to research the laws, procedures and policies governing your state courts or hire an attorney in the appropriate jurisdiction. In addition, unless otherwise noted, the procedural information conveyed is a composite of rules and regulations. While state law is uniform, the management of the courts may vary, depending on your jurisdiction. To determine the policies of your local court you may contact the clerk.

My hope is that the information you find herein will help you navigate the world of dispute resolution more smoothly.

Preventing

Clichés are phrases that we have heard all of our lives. There are five individual clichés with messages that seem appropriate to begin a discussion regarding the handling of adversarial situations. Haven't we all heard, "It takes two to argue"; "Cooler heads prevail"; "You can catch more bees with honey"; "You can win the battle but lose the war"; and "An ounce of prevention is worth a pound of cure?" All of them are mostly true, so why can't we live by them?

Practice each of the above and combine them with a belief in Murphy's Law: "Anything that can go wrong will go wrong," and you may be well on your way to minimizing the issues you will undoubtedly confront when purchasing or selling goods and services. But if it was really that easy we could tell most judges to take extended vacations, because it would be highly unlikely that potential litigants would ever see the inside of a courtroom.

A difficulty even the true believer of this mind-set faces is that one cannot control the character, attitude or ability of someone who could become your adversary in helping avoid or solve a problem. You will want to do all that you can to protect yourself, even before contacting the vendors of the goods or services you are contemplating purchasing.

When making a small purchase, like buying a meal at your favorite eatery, you want quality, value and service. Unless you get sick and can prove it was from the food served, if the restaurant fails in any of your expectations, you won't sue; you just won't return. Therefore, our focus will be on your larger purchases of goods and services. Buying a car or hiring a contractor to do work on your home are typical examples of transactions that require careful attention to prevent or minimize conflicts. Additionally, larger purchases generally require more time and attention in the decision-making process than buying a screw driver set at the Home Depot.

Before jumping into specifics, there is an underlying general principle that is inherent in doing business with which you should be familiar: *caveat emptor* (let the buyer beware.) In effect, it means that a buyer purchases a product at his or her own risk; that it is up to you to assess the quality of a product prior to the purchase. However, there are two exceptions to this

3

long-held doctrine: concealed latent defects to the product and material misrepresentation amounting to fraud. Of course, if you are bringing suit against a supplier of an alleged defective product, the burden is on you to prove either of these two conditions existed in order to win over a *caveat emptor* defense. I call this to your attention early in the prevention discussion because it is important for you be aware of these factors prior to entering into a contract. Due to the complex nature of a product failure lawsuit, it is advisable to consult with an attorney when contemplating or facing legal action.

When thinking about a purchase involving larger sums of money, significant personal time, or a high degree of risk, your first consideration should be **the selection of the right company or individual** with whom to do business. There are a number of criteria you may use in finding the people expected to serve you in an acceptable manner. Consider making a comprehensive list of the following criteria:

Capability - It is not always an easy task to make this evaluation when hiring someone for professional services. And yet, it is vital. The most obvious trait would be the company's track record. Years in business would certainly tell you something. One can assume that if the people have remained in business over a long period of time, providing the same service, they would in all probability pass this test.

Another way to gauge the company's capability is to talk with prior customers. Keep in mind the company will, in all probability, give you names of former customers that they have satisfied. Ask the past customers questions geared toward problems they may have experienced, and how they were resolved. Always ask if they would use the company again.

Reputation – Checking a company's reputation is very important prior to signing a contract. Asking people you trust for their recommendations is always a good start. Researching a company on the Internet is also advisable. You can use sites such as Angie's List, Facebook, and execute a Google search on the company itself. But you should take it a step further by checking with the Consumer Protection Agency in your state, the Better Business Bureau and consumer groups. You might also wish to check the courthouse in your local jurisdiction to see if there are any outstanding judgments against the company. It may require a visit to the courthouse to obtain this information.

Association Membership – In most professional fields, association membership is offered to companies and individuals working in their respective areas of specialization. Although affiliation with an association doesn't necessarily provide the general public with protection, it does indicate a company's desire to seek recognition as an upstanding member of that industry's community.

Additionally, most associations conduct educational programs that teach their members new techniques or the latest industry developments. As a customer of an affiliated company, the residual benefits of increased knowledge can have a positive impact for whatever transaction you are contemplating.

In some instances, associations will have a procedure for filing complaints about a member company. Some may provide mediation or arbitration services. Asking a prospective company which association(s) they belong to is a fair question.

Licensed – A check with various authorities, like the office of the Secretary of State, will tell you whether the company with which you're dealing is an active corporation, partnership, limited liability company, sole proprietorship, or other business entity. Beyond that, if you have contracted with someone to do a home project or repair, it is crucial that the individuals are properly licensed if the state or county requires licensure within the given specialty for which they are being hired such as plumbing and electrical work. In each case, the vendor should provide proof of his/her license.

It is highly recommended that you do business only with licensed companies or individuals.

Insured – Most businesses that are properly licensed also carry liability insurance. You do not want to risk having a claim against you or your insurance company if someone is injured on your property. Ask the company or individual to provide proof of their Liability and state-required Workers' Compensation policies, with adequate coverage, before contracting.

Financial Wherewithal – A company's financial viability is particularly difficult to ascertain. But, you at least want to be assured that if something does go wrong with the project or product you purchase, the company has the ability to make it right. This especially comes into play if you should end up facing them in court. Winning a case is one thing; collecting is another matter, but more about that subject later.

Other than reviewing, and being able to analyze, a company's financial statement, your options are limited as to the discovery of financial problems. You will be able to check a bankruptcy history with the proper agencies and should do so. At the very least, ask the company how it handles major errors such as painting a room the wrong color, installing a faulty product in your car, etc. Hopefully, you will get a satisfactory answer that may lend rise to language to be included in your contract. As a general rule, if a promise is not in the written contract, or provable in some other manner, it may not be binding.

Character and Personality – Perhaps the most subjective of these suggestions is measuring how your personality meshes with the people you are about to engage. This could be a key component of a successful relationship; particularly when trying to solve a disagreement after the work begins or ends. It is said that first impressions are lasting ones. If there is uneasiness with the contact people, stop and look elsewhere. Also, try not to be taken in by someone's effusive personality. Most sales people are in that profession because they can be very persuasive. That is not to say that you should be cynical; rather, look for genuineness in those individuals you are interviewing to engage in work.

Competitiveness – In most cases, your needs can be filled by more than one company. If you are buying a product or service that can be bid upon with the same specifications get competitive prices. Three bids seem to be most common in the business world.

Try to be as detailed as you can when working with the representatives of the companies. When the bids come in, compare them first to the specifications you gave each bidder. If items are missing, ask someone with authority at the company whether or not they are included. If the answer is yes, request that those items be confirmed in writing with a revised contract or a signed and dated addendum. If the items in question are not included, ask for a revised bid so that you will be comparing apples to apples with the other bids under consideration.

If one of the three bids is a good bit lower than the others, be cautious. Generally speaking, you get what you pay for in the market place. On the other hand, the company with the lowest bid may have a lower overhead and/or buys products at a lower cost. The company may be in greater need of work than the others, or simply has made a mistake. If all the other criteria are acceptable, and you are comfortable with the lowest bidder, discuss their price with them. You don't necessarily have to share the other bids, but ask them to review their numbers. Once verified, you may wish to proceed with the lowest bidder.

Some people will disclose the low bid to the other bidding companies, hoping for an even lower price from at least one of them. From an ethical point of view, I am not in favor of this approach. However, the exception might be with a company that you have used before and feel such a loyalty toward that you would like to give them another opportunity to review their bid. But, unless you are very familiar with and totally trust the higher bidder, consider that a subsequent severe price cut might come back to haunt you someway, somehow. This is especially likely if there are many blind items to be used in the servicing of the project.

Once you have reviewed the quotations from all three bidders and they all run higher than you thought or could afford, you may wish to speak with your first choice and let them know what your budget is. They may be willing to rework the specifications to get you what you want, and have the project become affordable.

Production Schedule – Assuming a company meets all the other criteria to your satisfaction, the project start date or product delivery date very often will impact your decision. Before selecting your second choice because of a disappointing schedule from company number one, think hard about the impact of waiting. If the time frame is at all livable, your best bet might be to wait and go with the company which appears to meet all your other needs. On the other hand, that decision might depend on how close your second choice is in your analysis, and whether or not they are able to meet your requirements in a more timely fashion.

Product Availability – Quite often a company may not have a part or product needed for a job in their inventory or available at their distributor when needed. As with the aforementioned Production Schedule delay, you may be faced with a similar decision, whether or not to change from your first choice company to another or wait until the part or product becomes available. This decision would depend on your comfort level with the alternate. If there is any doubt, it may be in your best interest to wait it out or accept a substitute product that is available and remain with your first choice.

Return Policy – When purchasing a product, the establishment's return policy should be at the top of the list when selecting a vendor. Larger companies, like chain stores, all have firm, but generally fair return policies. It is important for you to understand the terms of these policies and conform to them when returning merchandise. Only under rare circumstances will the major retailers break their own policies when it comes to giving you your money back or offering a store credit. In these atypical cases, most often it will take a management decision to break a store policy.

There have been occasional cases where a consumer sues a major retailer in small claims court. In virtually all these lawsuits, the store is represented by an attorney who brings to court all the documentation to support his/her client's position. It is not impossible for a consumer to win, but it is a steep uphill battle. To avoid confrontation in these circumstances, it is always best to conform to the store's return policy.

With "mom and pop" businesses, ask for the return policy in writing. Even a hand written entry on the sales slip, signed by the owner or manager, can be most helpful should a dispute arise.

When it comes to returning merchandise bought on the Internet, the consumer is faced with issues quite different from dealing with a local store. That is not to suggest that those types of sellers are unscrupulous. In fact, most reputable Internet firms post their return policies somewhere on their Web-site. Most companies use a Return Merchandise Authorization (RMA) form they send to buyers to make it easier for the purchaser to send back the merchandise. If you determine there is a problem with whatever you bought, ask the company to send you an RMA form. Note that not all companies use an RMA method and that every company that does has its own way of providing this form. Prior to purchase, be certain to find out who pays for the shipping when returning merchandise, and ask if there is a restocking fee.

It is extremely difficult to sue an Internet company in small claims court and because on-line sales are growing each year, it also increases your risks. One major source of consumer protection for Internet buying comes from your credit card company. American Express is particularly good at supporting its card holders when a dispute arises. Master Card, Visa, and Discover can be helpful as well, but the consumer bears more of the burden to prove who was at fault with the transaction in question. To help resolve disputes between its buyers and sellers, eBay and other on-line auction companies offer mediation services. In all cases, be extra cautious when making your purchases on-line, by phone or mail-in coupon.

***

An analysis of the cases I see in small claims court clearly shows that the majority of disputes fall into one the following broad categories: **Automobile Purchases; Automobile Repairs; Home Services; Landlord/Tenant; Employment; Collection; Home Owners Association; Professional Services; Technology Services; Service Contracts and Cohabitation Dissolution**. In each of these categories, there are unique sets of circumstances that repeatedly surface between the disputing parties. For this reason, it is helpful to discuss the most common issues of conflict that appear with regularity either in court or during mediation conferences.

(Another major segment of cases heard in small claims court are those involving personal injury. In virtually every case that I have seen in the courtroom, the plaintiffs and defendants have been represented by attorneys. Because I have not conducted a significant number of personal injury mediations, I cannot offer specific help in this specialized field.)

AUTOMOBILE PURCHASES

NEW CARS – Next to purchasing a home, buying a car is generally the largest expenditure most people make. Rarely have I spoken with a person who says that they have enjoyed the experience. To help reduce anxiety and avoid conflict, it may be helpful to examine the major elements within the sales contract for a new car.

New cars are almost always purchased from manufacturers' franchised dealerships. Other than issues concerning the price, trade-in, financing, delivery, etc., buyers are always protected by the standard warranties offered by all manufacturers regarding the performance and quality of the car, including defects that appear upon or after delivery of the car. There are also federal and state protections offered to consumers purchasing new automobiles.

The Magnuson-Moss Warranty Act is the federal "Lemon Law." Georgia, like many other states, has the Georgia Lemon Law. In both cases these laws provide compensation to consumers of defective automobiles, trucks, motorcycles, RV's, boats, computers, and appliances. Based on information furnished by the State of Georgia, "you must generally have a product that suffered multiple repair attempts under the manufacturer's factory warranty." It also states that, "Lemon Law compensation can include a refund, replacement or cash compensation."

Should you find yourself in a situation from which a new car is defective, in your opinion, and you can't get satisfaction from the dealership where the car was purchased, the next step should be to contact the manufacturer's regional office. If there is merit to your complaint, chances are very high that the problem will be resolved at that level. Assuming you have still not been satisfied, it is recommended that you speak with an attorney who has successfully handled Lemon Law cases.

Misunderstandings with new car dealerships often arise once the decision is made to make the purchase. When you look at the bottom-line price, always ask for the *drive-out* price. There are a number of other components on the sales contract that impact the actual *drive-out* price. Often they tend to make the negotiation confusing, frustrating, and emotional.

Once you believe you have a deal, the salesperson at the dealership will undoubtedly have a sales contract prepared by the business office. Typically, the top portion, below the buyer's name, address, and insurance information, describes the new car in detail. If there is a trade-in vehicle, that too will be described in a similar matter. In addition, the conditions of the sale are in the small print on the front and back of the contract. Even though it is a lot to read, take the time to do so. If you have any questions, get answers before completing the transaction.

All conditions regarding the money will be itemized, usually along the bottom half of the right side.

The top line dollar figure represents the Manufacturer's Suggested Retail Price (MSRP). On some contracts this line item will be called the," Base Price". It should match the price on the sticker adhered to the window of the exact car you are buying. Using that top line dollar figure as a basis, the items below should reflect all the monetary conditions of the sale that you have negotiated.

In some cases, at your request, the dealer will be installing additional items, e.g. chrome wheels, etc. These add-ons will be described and their associated additional costs will be listed below the base price.

Most often the next dollar figure you will see is the "Selling Price." That will be calculated by adding the costs of the installed items to the base price, minus any discount you may have negotiated. Should the deal include a trade-in, the amount of money you are being offered by the dealer, called "trade allowance," will be reflected on the next line.

Preprinted on many new cars sales contracts is an item often referred to as "Administrative Fee", which is usually in the hundreds of dollars. If you ask about it, you will be told that it reflects an overhead cost for the dealership. Because this added cost to you appears after you thought you had a deal, conflict surfaces. Whether this is negotiable is between the sales people and you. I mention it here so that you may anticipate this unexpected added cost and deal with it earlier in the process.

The only remaining costs to you in a cash deal should be the sales tax and a small charge for tags and title. At the end of the process, the most important dollar figure to you on the entire contract is the "Balance Due On Delivery" which was described earlier as your drive out price. A clear understanding of this number before the contract is put in final form will make this major purchase a great deal more pleasant.

CERTIFIED PRE-OWNED CARS (CPO) - As a general rule, the chance of getting into a legal entanglement in small claims court over the purchase of a CPO is relatively the same as with a new car; very slim. But, as with any sales contract, there are precautions you should take.

The concept for CPO cars began in the late 1980s by Mercedes Benz as a marketing incentive to make their luxury cars more affordable. Also, it was deemed an excellent opportunity to build brand loyalty. It worked so well that other luxury brands offered similar programs shortly thereafter. Today, most car manufacturers offer some type of CPO program.

The criteria used to determine whether a car can be a CPO is based on age, mileage, and condition. Each manufacturer has its own standards for qualifying a vehicle for its program.

A key assumption you may make when choosing a CPO car is that it has been inspected, repaired (if necessary), and warranted.

The inspection phase in the certification process also varies with manufacturers and dealers. Some advertise that their CPO's have a 112 point inspection, some 200, and even a few claim 300. In virtually all cases, you will be provided a copy of the checklist which outlines every point of examination.

With regard to repairs, you can assume the dealer pre-screened the car when accepting it on a trade. Those that do not appear to qualify are sold without a CPO designation, disposed of at auction, or wholesaled in another manner. The checklist will clearly point out which repairs have to be made. Some of them might qualify under the time and mileage remaining with the new-car warranty. Other unanticipated repairs that are not covered will be done at the dealer's cost or the car may be pulled from the program. Your comfort level concerning the condition of the car at this point should be fairly high.

It is very important to carefully consider the warranty of a CPO car. There is a major difference between a factory-backed program and a dealer certified program. With a factory-backed program, repairs that qualify under the warranty can be made at any franchised dealer in the country. This is more than a convenience, especially when travelling out of town. Another significant benefit is that it comes with the purchase of the car, at no additional cost.

A dealer certified program almost always requires you to have repairs done at the dealership where you bought the car. For those drivers who rarely leave town, this program might be perfectly acceptable.

A number of third party sellers offer extended warranties, which must be very carefully examined before purchase. Determining which repair centers will honor the warranty must be clearly understood in advance. Sometimes, consumers are attracted to these companies by very attractive prices, but be exceptionally cautious when doing business with an unknown, usually out of town, purveyor of auto warranty repair policies.

Costs for factory-backed CPO automobiles can run anywhere from 2%-8% of the selling price and are built into the asking price. Dealer programs generally run less and are handled as an add-on. Costs can be based on a sliding scale, depending on the length of the warranty (e.g. 36 months/50,000 miles or some other combination of months and miles)

Another major component to these CPO programs that must be considered is the type of CPO warranty you are getting. Essentially, there are two: "Bumper-To-Bumper" or "Drive Train."

All new cars and the majority of factory-backed CPO car come with a bumper-to-bumper warranty. In effect, it means that the costs for parts and labor for any repair, other than items that wear out with use such as brakes and tires will be covered. There are conditions to be met on the buyer's part, but that varies with each policy.

Drive Train warranties include: engine, transmission, drive axle, and four-wheel or all-wheel drive (if applicable.) Usually, it will also include 24/7 road side assistance, in addition to some other options.

If your car is to be financed, and you meet all the credit qualifications, quite often a CPO deal can yield a more favorable interest rate on the loan.

Be certain to consider the following when buying a CPO car: review the certification check list; require a repair and maintenance history be furnished to you. If there is time left on the new car warranty, get a clear understanding as to the terms.

Also, read the fine print in all paperwork associated with the purchase.

Most dealers and large retailers offer a large inventory of non-CPO cars. Similar consideration should be given to their purchase.

USED CARS – As the topic of used cars encompasses a wide array of automobiles beyond CPO cars, for discussion purposes **newer** used cars with an approximate age range of six years and fewer than 100,000 miles will be separated from those even **older** and with a higher mileage.

Assuming the buyer of a **newer** used car has a comprehensive diagnostic done by a reliable mechanic, is purchasing the car from a trustworthy seller, and determines that the car has a clean history, the risk of being faced with immediate and/or costly repairs is greatly diminished. In spite of these conditions, however, there are further steps a buyer can take to increase their confidence level.

Ideally, a sought-after car can be located at an authorized dealer of the same brand. Better yet, if the specific car you are considering was acquired by them through trade, personnel at the dealership had an opportunity to thoroughly examine the car and talk to the previous owner prior to accepting it.

A second best option is to buy a newer used car from an authorized dealer of another brand. Other than the familiarity factor with a dealer of the same brand, the benefits are pretty much the same.

A close third option is a purchase from a company like CARMAX, which is a national chain. Their advantage above others is a huge inventory, a seven day return policy, and an excellent warranty program at reasonable prices. To their credit, CARMAX also was the first major retail car company to establish a "no haggle pricing" policy. That concept has now been adopted by dealerships nationwide.

A common thread between these three options is that all their cars will go through a safety inspection, at a minimum, before being offered for sale. Also, in virtually every case, dealerships are quite concerned with maintaining a reputation for integrity and ethical business practices.

Whichever type of dealership you choose, also keep in mind the sales tax advantage of trading your current car as part of the deal. As an illustration, if the car being purchased is $25,000, the trade-in price is $5,000, and the sales tax rate in your area is 7%, you will be taxed $1,400 based on the $20,000 difference. If you sold the car privately, your tax on the new purchase is based on the full $25,000, and thus, amounts to $1,750. In other words, to breakeven, you must receive $5,350 from the party buying your car.

The purchase of an **older**, higher mileage car is an entirely different challenge than that of a new, CPO, or newer used vehicle. If the potential for mechanical or electronic failure is a possibility with a newer pre-owned car, it is a probability with an older car. Too often, I conduct mediations with buyers whose expectations were that of driving off the lot with a new car. If you approach the purchase with an understanding that problems with the car may very well surface soon after you own the car, there are many ways you can maximize your satisfaction with the purchase.

To begin with, you may take the risk of buying a used car at auction (if you are licensed to do so); from a used car dealer; from a private party advertising on Auto Trader, Craigslist, classified ad, sign on a parked vehicle, etc.; or from a personal friend or relative. There are common precautions associated with each of these approaches, and a number of facts that should be noted to avoid conflict. At the same time, there are a number of singular facets that should also be noted to prevent a dispute.

Dealer Purchases - Like many other industries comprised of small enterprises, you will experience every type of owner and salesperson, from hard working and honest individuals to the unscrupulous. If ever *caveat emptor* should be applied, it is here. My objective is to keep you and the selling party out of court. With apologies to the "good guys," my prospective is from the negative side of the used-car business.

A common sales technique employed by some of the "bad guys" is known as ***Bait and Switch.*** This is a method to lure you to their car lot by advertising a deal that sounds too good to be true. And it usually is! By the time you arrive to see the car, you are told that it has been sold. At that point, the pressure mounts from a salesperson by coaxing you into buying a different car of lesser value for the same money or a more expensive car than you were considering.

Another shady sales approach that is to your disadvantage is called *"Spot Delivery,"* which is another name for a *"Yo-Yo"* sale. It doesn't matter what it is called because either term creates the same problem. It works like this when the last step in the sale is financing. Immediately after signing all the documents but without running a credit check, the salesperson hands you the keys. You are probably thinking that the car is yours and you drive away. A day or so later, you get a call from the dealer stating that your credit has been turned down. You are told to bring the car back, where a new, less beneficial deal is renegotiated. Most buyers will go along and agree to a revised deal they initially would not have considered. This situation can be complicated if you had a trade-in and the dealer tells you it has been sold. To avoid the "Spot Delivery" or "Yo-Yo" spin, ask for credit approval in writing before taking delivery or leave the car with the dealer until it has been confirmed.

"Odometer Fraud" is another trick in some dealer's playbook. You may be considering a car that unbeknownst to you has many more miles than indicated on the dashboard panel. To avoid this rip-off, ask to see the title long before making your final decision. If there is a discrepancy leave that lot and never to return. In some cases, the title of a car at auction may not have transferred to the dealer's name. Under those circumstances verifying the mileage may be impossible at the time of purchase.

With millions of wrecked cars being sold each year, a buyer must watch out for *"Salvage Title Fraud."* Disclosure of a salvage title is a requirement in many states. In Georgia, for instance, any car built after 1993, requires the owner to file for a Salvage Title Application if the car was declared a total loss by an insurance company. There are a number of scams common to the selling of salvage vehicles, such as *"Title Washing"* where a car is moved to a state that has looser application rules and has the car registered in that state. Another is *"Car Clipping"* where the front and back ends of two cars are welded together.

Many buyers knowingly buy salvaged vehicles. They are attracted by the low price, feel they have the mechanical background to deal with potential problems, and are obviously willing to take the risk. Even those buyers have to find insurance companies who will write a policy for a salvage vehicle, most often at a much higher premium.

Always ask the seller to show you the title to determine if the vehicle has been salvaged. Somewhere on the title there should be wording such as salvaged, totaled, rebuilt, reconditioned, etc. Should you find out after buying the car that it was salvaged and it wasn't disclosed up front by the seller, you may have a *cause of action* (the fact(s) that gives a party the right to seek judicial redress or relief against another) and file a lawsuit. As with all civil suits, the burden will be on the person who brings the lawsuit to prove that the seller knew and hid this information from a buyer.

Unless your sales contract specifically allows for a trial period, you cannot simply return a car and demand your money back. While the State of Georgia does have a "Right of Rescission" law, it only pertains to real estate loans. Another often misunderstood Georgia statute has to do with a 72 hour "cooling off" period. That law provides protection only for purchases from a door-to-door salesperson. On the other hand, if you can prove that the dealer committed *fraud* (intention to deceive, false representation of a matter of fact) you may get relief in court. Proving it becomes the challenge, especially for someone without a legal background.

Notwithstanding nasty practices used by some car dealers, there are actions you can take when considering the purchase of the older, higher-mileage, less-expensive car to assure yourself that you are getting what you pay for and avoid conflict.

After carefully looking over both the exterior and interior of the car, take it for a test drive on city streets and an expressway or major highway. Make note of every unusual noise or occurrence, like the car pulling to the left or right. (If you think that this advice is elementary, I have had many cases in mediation where the buyer merely started the car up and, without test driving it, made the decision to buy it.) Whether you agree to purchase the vehicle with the noises or other detectable problems, or trust the dealer to fix them is totally up to you. For my money, I would immediately continue looking for another car. There are many undetectable problems with a used car that only a professional can uncover. One way to absolutely minimize the risk of purchasing a problem automobile is to take it to a mechanic for a thorough diagnostic test prior to finalizing a deal. Costs range from about $75 to $150, depending on the comprehensiveness of the test. A top flight inspector hired to do a bumper to bumper test will not only cover items like mechanical and electrical problems, but will be able to find water damage, frame damage, parts that have been repainted or replaced, and a variety of other problems. If the dealer is reluctant to allow you to leave the lot with the car to get this done, there are mobile auto inspection companies that will come to the site where the car is located. If the dealer won't allow you to have any professional inspection done, that's a red flag. Under those circumstances, you should probably leave the car lot immediately. Remind yourself that you spending hard-earned money, and there are many other cars available that you will like just as well. In other words, don't get emotionally attached to one car and buy it even though it may give you a major headache down the road.

Assuming you decide to pursue a particular car, haggling over price and financing terms is the next step. How good a bargainer you are and the flexibility of the dealer vary widely; these two components are based on circumstance and the moment. If you are a cash buyer and the dealer needs the sale, you may be in the strongest position for a favorable deal.

Remember, there is no shortage of used cars and the dealer is anxious to move each vehicle off the lot so that he can make his profit and either go to auction and buy its replacement or secure another trade-in.

When you decide to buy a car and the price is firmly established, be certain that the verbally agreed upon price is reflected on the bill of sale, and make sure to read all of the small print on both sides of the document. The time to resolve all outstanding issues regarding the purchase is *before* signing anything. Once you are completely satisfied, you can proceed with executing the contract.

Most older, high-mileage used cars will be purchased on an *"as-is"* basis. Those words will probably appear on the window sticker and most likely in the fine print on the bill of sale. Those are two small words that have enormous implications when buying a car, motorcycle, boat, recreation vehicle, etc. It means that the product is being purchased in its existing condition. It gives notice that the risk of the purchase is the buyer's, especially if the vehicle or other mechanical product was made available for inspection.

There are a significant amount of cases that show up in court over "as-is" issues. Unfortunately for the buyer, the judge's hands are frequently tied if the buyer signed a contract with an "as-is" condition. There have been cases where a car will break down before the buyer gets it home and finds him or herself on the losing side in a lawsuit. Unless you can prove that the seller was aware of hidden defects or had made certain assertions about the condition of the vehicle, a ruling will most often go against you.

The best way to avoid a dispute arising from an "as-is" legal action is to negotiate the best deal you can before the purchase. Many reputable used-car dealers will agree to a short-term warranty, perhaps thirty to sixty days. Hidden defects or inherent problems with the vehicle should surface within the first few weeks of ownership.

Some dealers might offer a longer-term warranty for a fee. If it is available to you, be sure it is in writing and the terms are distinctly spelled out. *Never rely on verbal commitments.* A key condition to watch out for with a warranty is whether it covers all parts and labor. Also, consider the remedies if the car can't be fixed to your satisfaction. In some cases, the warranty states that you can get your money back. This arrangement is clear-cut if a trade-in wasn't part of the deal.

In some cases, the dealer may only offer you a replacement vehicle of equal value. However, you may have to settle for a car you don't like. If this turns out to be the arrangement, be sure to get a warranty on the replacement car, too.

Whichever warranty you agree to, it is better than buying the car "as-is." At least you will have some comfort and relief if the car breaks down during the warranty period. If the dealer fails to live up to his or her end of the bargain, you will have meaningful evidence to present if the resulting dispute goes to court.

Private Party (Stranger) – A significant percentage of used cars is purchased from individuals who advertise in some fashion. Choosing to buy a car from someone you don't know can present greater risks than from a licensed used-car dealer. Even in consideration of the precautions we covered, with an established car lot you might have recourse or options should problems arise. The owner of the business may be quite ethical and his or her reputation might be of concern. With a private party, in all probability you won't have the option to work out a favorable outcome to a dispute without suing the seller. In addition, the opportunity for any type of warranty is generally surrendered when purchasing a vehicle from a private party.

Assuming you decide to purchase an automobile from a stranger, follow the same general guidelines that are applicable to buying a used car from a dealer, as stated previously.

Many individuals claim to be selling their personal cars when they are actually masking a side business. If they obtain a proper business license, there is nothing illegal about it. However, the concern for you as the buyer of a car from one of these individuals is that they know very little about the car. Usually, they will bid on a car at auction venues, so it would stand to reason that they gave it a cursory look. The way the business works, however, there is little or no time for anything like a diagnostic test. To a great extent, it is the buyer's gamble when cars are purchased in this manner, and that gamble becomes yours when you take title.

When discussing the car with the seller, it is fair to ask how long he or she has owned the car. The answer you receive may or may not affect your decision, but at least you will have a better idea of what you are buying.

Before giving the seller any money, be sure you are getting a clean, unencumbered title. A legitimate title will show if there are any lien holders. Also, it is preferable to personally witness the seller signing the title over to you. But that is only one half of the transaction. A bill of sale should accompany the title. You will not only need it for protection, should a legal action follow this purchase, but you may need it to show a police officer if you get stopped prior to getting license plates. The signature of the seller should be on the bill of sale and on the title. There was a recent court case in which the seller's brother signed the bill of sale because the seller wasn't home when the transaction took place. It became an issue for the judge to consider.

Private Party (Friend or Relative) – The good news for those buying a car from a friend or relative is that the condition of the car is almost always a known quantity. The presumption is that the car is truly the seller's personal car. You will know why the car is being sold. You will be told of any problems with the car in advance. The last thing on the mind of the seller is to take advantage of you. Both of you may have even checked the value of the car on Kelly Blue Book (www.kbb.com), Edmunds' (www.edmunds.com) or NADA (www.nadaguides.com).

All of this makes it sound like the ideal situation, and it could be. But the problem is that due to the relationship between buyer and seller, many of the requisites for making the sale a sound business transaction are overlooked or skipped. Doing it the right way should be paramount regardless of how close the parties are on a personal level. Avoid problems ahead of time and both the buyer and seller will be more comfortable.

***

For those people who do not feel knowledgeable enough, are intimidated by the process, or simply do not have the time to buy a car on their own, using a car broker may be a viable option. These individuals serve solely as middlemen who will search for the make, model, and year car you are seeking, new or used. Some will also assist in the selling of your current car. Based on feedback that I have received, the range of fee arrangements appear to be from a flat percentage of the purchase or sales price to a flat fee of several hundred dollars. They assume no responsibility for the quality of the car itself; that remains between the buyer and seller.

***

No discussion regarding the purchase of a used car should come to a conclusion without mentioning CARFAX (www.carfax.com), the leading vehicle history report company. Founded in 1985, the company now serves consumers and dealers in the U.S. and Canada.

CARFAX offers free reports, but they are limited in scope. More detailed reports are available for a fee. There are three general areas upon which they report:
1. Title Problems (severe accidents, lemons, floods, and odometer problems)
2. Ownership History (how many previous owners, mileage, rental or fleet car)
3. Accidents (if there was a total loss declared by an insurance company, air bag deployment, frame damage, service records)

As an alternative to CARFAX, many buyers are using AutoCheck, a company offering similar services for more than ten years. They claim to offer a more comprehensive menu of services, but at a higher cost. AutoCheck can be researched on their web-site (www.autocheck.com).

You are urged to always pull a CARFAX and/or AutoCheck report for any used car you are considering buying.

***

Financing

More than 70% of new vehicles and 40% of used cars are financed, which present a number of issues that could impact your decision-making when purchasing a vehicle. The objective in this section is to provide information that may minimize conflict, reduce stress and increase satisfaction when borrowing a significant amount of money.

The primary concerns of most buyers who will be financing are:
1. The total dollar amount to be financed
2. The interest rate on the loan
3. The number of months or years it will take to pay off the loan
4. The dollar amount of the monthly payment

However, sometimes overlooked are terms and conditions in the fine print of the financing agreement. These may include early payoff penalties, late fees, repossession charges, collection expenses, and an assortment of other contract clauses.

The amount being financed should reflect the negotiated, final "drive-out" price. That dollar figure becomes the starting point for the loan that will impact the rate of interest and the number of months being financed.

Interest rates will vary depending on a number of factors, including:
1. The creditworthiness of the borrower
2. The type, age and condition of the car
3. The dollar amount of the down payment
4. The rates offered at the bank, credit union, finance company, or dealer (in-house financing)
5. Dealer incentive promotions that may be offered at the time of purchase.

The specific rate of interest being charged to the borrower should be clearly indicated on the loan agreement. In some states there may be no limit to the interest rate a financing source may charge. Some states set a maximum legal rate; that information is readily available to the public and should be researched prior to signing a loan agreement.

I have conducted mediations that involved disputes in a used-car purchase where the loan documents indicated total interest charges that exceeded the price of the car. However, it is certainly the borrower's decision to determine what is acceptable. My objective in addressing this subject is to raise the awareness of borrowers so that they clearly understand how much interest they will be paying for a car loan prior to signing a contract.

Due to personal financial considerations, many buyers prefer to stretch out payments for as long as possible. Loan terms are being offered and accepted for as long as ninety-six months. These long-term payouts may appear to be attractive when initially making the loan because the monthly payments are lower; however, there are pitfalls. First, interest rates are often higher with a long-term loan. Second, the total dollars paid by the buyer for the car and the loan, when all costs are taken into account, may be much more than originally contemplated. Also, the value of the vehicle will almost always depreciate because of age, mileage and the condition of the car. The value of the vehicle actually may be less than the loan balance when trading it in for another car. It may require cash to pay off the old loan or increase the amount being borrowed on the replacement vehicle. What may have seemed attractive at the outset may not have been the best decision in the long run.

There is one specific lesser-noticed term in many loan agreements that surfaces in mediation cases relative to repossession. Once the car is back in the hands of the lender, he or she may sell it at any price deemed reasonable. The borrower in all probability will be responsible for the loan balance, plus other allowable repossession charges. In one mediation case I handled, the borrower believed that because she returned the car voluntarily, it was not considered repossessed. The case went to trial and the judge ruled in favor of the lender. If the borrower understood the rules earlier, she may have chosen another option.

Borrowers can avoid conflict by making an informed decision after thoroughly reading the terms and conditions of the loan agreement, making all payments in a timely fashion and possibly renegotiating the loan. Sadly, the courts are full of cases where these preventative steps were not taken.

***

Leasing

The concept of leasing cars actually began when the Model T Ford was still the most popular car riding the roads of America in the 1920s. It took until the late 1980s and early 1990s, when there was an upsurge in the cost of buying an automobile, for many car owners to turn to the fast-growing trend of leasing. Today, approximately 20% of new cars are being leased.

Companies view leasing as an advantage over purchasing due to tax advantages that allow a write-off of the total lease payment. Consumers find leasing attractive because they can get into a more expensive car at a perceived lower monthly payment.

The following information may help consumers avoid misunderstandings and disputes when considering a leasing arrangement:

- The lessee does not own the car; the leasing company does. Therefore, it can dictate how to use, maintain and insure the car.
- Leasing contracts are often more stringent than purchasing and financing agreements.
- Many leases require a substantial dollar payment due at signing. When comparing a lease versus a purchase, this should be a major consideration.
- Advertised lease payments often do not include sales taxes. In some cases, you could be paying sales tax on the full value of the car but not getting the benefit of its full use.
- Leases have pre-set mileage limits. The penalty for driving more than the mileage allowed in the contract can be very expensive.

- Unless you are the type of person who keeps a car in pristine condition, leasing may not be a practical option. There are contractual requirements pertaining to the condition of the car when the lease is terminated that should be clearly understood in the beginning. Charges for body damage, tears or stains to the interior or perhaps mismatched tires must be paid to the leasing company at the end of the lease.

- It is entirely possible that the leasing company will require you to buy more expensive insurance than you would for a car you purchased and financed. They may not allow a policy with a deductible, as an example.

- Most leasing companies will offer the lessee an option to purchase the car at the end of the lease. If that is your goal, you should clearly understand in advance what the price, often referred to as the "residual," will be at that future date.

- Very often the payments for a long-term lease may not be much lower than for a purchase. You may wish to do a comparison prior to making a final decision.

- It may be very difficult or expensive to terminate a lease early. However, if your lease is transferable, a computer search can locate companies that provide services that may help you accomplish this.

An old cliché asserts, "All that glitters isn't gold"; hence, it would be wise to thoroughly research all aspects of a car lease prior to signing a contract. If after doing so, you are satisfied that all your requirements are met, you may move forward with a higher degree of comfort.

AUTOMOBILE REPAIRS

A hefty percentage of lawsuits in small claims court are over issues regarding car repairs. Many of the cases involve vehicles that have been driven for well over a hundred thousand miles, may not have been properly maintained and may have had multiple owners.

Although they vary, a majority of automobile complaints that wind up in court are related to engines or transmissions. In both instances, the disputes stem from either a misunderstanding as to what the quote included or a repair that was alleged to have been faulty. A detailed quotation, signed and dated by the mechanic, could clear up many issues before work begins.

In deference to the honest, hard-working mechanics, at times undetected additional problems surface after a proper repair has been completed. As a result, additional money may be needed for parts and labor to make the car drivable in a satisfactory and durable condition. Hearing the bad news from the mechanic or discovering the problem after the initial repairs were paid for frequently causes friction and anger by the car's owner. Quite often, there is a prevailing attitude that the mechanic should have known prior to quoting the job. These are circumstances where each party may have a point. Trying to calmly work out a solution is to everyone's benefit before either party takes it to the next level.

Most of the automobile cases that I have mediated concern problems with either the motor or the transmission.

Engines – If a car is in otherwise good shape, replacing a worn out engine may constitute a wise dollar-and-cents' decision to add useable life.

Assuming an engine is beyond repair, there are three options the owner can take:
1. Purchase a new one, although that alternative is usually quite costly.
2. Purchase a remanufactured or rebuilt engine.
3. Purchase a used one, which may be the least advantageous of these alternatives.

Before moving forward with option #2, the more information you can accumulate will help you make the most beneficial decision. By doing a computer search under "rebuilt engines" or something similar, you can access professional associations that specifically deal with remanufactured or rebuilt engines. These organizations exist to educate the consumer about the economic and environmental benefits in purchasing those kinds of engines.

If money is the overriding issue in making a decision, the purchase of a used engine may be the only answer. However, a buyer must be aware that purchasing a used engine will not allow him or his mechanic to know the engine's history, including how many miles are on it or whether it has been in a serious wreck. To ameliorate concerns, it is suggested that you insist on a warranty from your mechanic. His or her supplier may offer one or you may have to rely solely on the mechanic.

Whether you are buying a remanufactured, rebuilt or used engine, it is important to clarify at the outset which party is responsible for costs associated with pulling out the old engine and the cost to install the replacement engine. Typically, the supplier of the engine does not cover removal or installation charges. Labor expenditures in these circumstances have been issues we have attempted to resolve in mediations more than a few times.

Transmissions – A malfunctioning transmission can sometimes be repaired depending on how damaged it is. Fixing it depends on the mechanic's analysis of the extent of damage. If he feels it is repairable, that should be the least expensive and quickest way to get you rolling again. A confident and reliable mechanic should be willing to give you at least a short-term warranty on his work.

As with engines, if a transmission is irreparable you are left with three choices: purchase a new, rebuilt or used one. To assure maximum satisfaction, it is always better to choose a new transmission. However, very often the age and condition of the car does not justify the cost. The second best route is the purchase of a rebuilt transmission. While the warranty may not offer the same protection as one with a new transmission, at least you will receive a degree of assurance in writing. The third option, a used transmission, is risky. Most mechanics will generally steer you away from a used transmission because they can be so unreliable.

Disputes over transmission repairs frequently arise due to an initial misdiagnosis. Although I do not have mechanical expertise, I hear so many cases where the problem was not the transmission itself but something else that caused the transmission to go bad. The unfortunate part is that the other problem could not have been detected until the transmission was replaced. In many of these cases, the mechanic may not be held responsible for a hidden problem. If additional work needs to be done to totally correct the problem, a negotiated compromise for additional costs is recommended.

HOME SERVICES

In my mediating experience, disputes about services performed at one's home run a close second to automobile purchases or repairs. Where there is a cluster of similar lawsuits, certain patterns emerge. Most disagreements with repairmen or contractors are about money, the quality of workmanship or an incomplete job. The home services cases we see in court range from plumbing to lawn maintenance to just about everything, but the majority of the complaints are either with home remodeling or roofing.

There are different ways to prevent home services' disputes:

REMODELING – The cost of most remodeling projects typically exceeds the $15,000 maximum award amount allowed in Georgia's small claims courts, so the amounts sought are generally for only a portion of the total contract amount. (Note that the maximum dollar amount in small claims court varies by states.)

Previously, we discussed the criteria for selecting the right company with which to do business. Assuming you use those as a guideline, here are several additional recommendations prior to seeking bids for your project:

1. Get complete agreement from each party who has to live with and/or pay for the remodeling. Based on my experience, it is vitally important to have all aspects of what is envisioned discussed thoroughly before beginning. Not only will this help get the project started on the right foot, but it could very well avoid costly changes made in progress.

2. Budget permitting, hire an architect who can blend your concept with his or her own, and provide you with renderings and blueprints which conform to local building codes. Builders can then prepare more accurate bids.

3. Engage an interior designer who can also play a significant preliminary and ongoing role. One can be extremely helpful in not only helping you with selecting accessories, paint colors, wallpaper, etc., but can also help you select the builder by joining you when interviewing contractors.

If the scope of the project does not warrant the extra help or the budget won't allow for it, most remodeling companies can provide drawings and code-approved plans based on your verbally expressed visualization.

After choosing the contractor with the most acceptable bid, carefully review the proposal. It should describe each phase of the work in detail. Brand names and model numbers for all products selected, like appliances, must be itemized. Where allowances are concerned, such as carpeting or cabinets, make sure the dollars allocated are sufficient for the quality you are seeking.

Many remodeling contracts require the home owner to purchase the products and/or materials. The benefits to you are many:

- You will know exactly what you are paying.
- You may be eliminating additional mark-ups by your builder.
- You will deal directly with the suppliers.

- It will enable you to ask questions and make changes on the spot, if necessary, to replace discontinued or out-of-stock items.

The negative side is that the responsibility of providing the exact products, materials and specifications shifts from the builder to you. Very often the specifications are exact components and measurements, and it takes a professional talking to a professional to get it right.

There is also the matter of transporting the products and/or materials to your home or business which can usually be arranged by the supplier. Obviously, many items are too large or too heavy to transport without a truck. You may also be responsible for having the products and/or materials on-site by a certain date to keep crews working. Delays could run up costs and negatively impact the stated completion date. If the builder agrees to handle all pick-ups, it should be stated in the contract.

Another method of doing business with a contractor is on a cost-plus basis whereby the builder is required to charge you only for his direct costs for labor and materials, plus an agreed-upon mark-up on the total amount. The materials portion is easier to account for because you will receive copies of all receipts. Unless you are paying the workers directly, you will have to trust the contractor that the information provided to you will be true and accurate. Working on this basis is more time-consuming for the home owner and is suggested to only those people who are well-organized in record-keeping.

Other contracts are priced with firm quotes. The only additional costs will be for changes made to the specifications. This is the easiest way to do business for the home owner. Because there is more risk for the builder the price could be somewhat higher because the builder may include additional dollars to cover unforeseen costs.

All contracts for remodeling should contain proof of the contractor's state license and number, and evidence of liability and Workers' Compensation insurance. Insist that language be included that all work meets building codes of the local jurisdiction. Additionally, acquiring the proper permits for a project will give you the comfort of knowing that all legal and safety requirements are met. Failing to do so can cause severe problems for both you and your contractor, including fines and possibly the removal of any non-permitted construction.

Some property owners require their contractor to provide a performance bond prior to any construction. This instrument, issued by an insurance company or a bank, helps assure satisfactory completion of a project. It is most commonly used for new construction or sizable renovations.

If the completion date is important to you, a projected time frame stated in the contract would be a necessity. However, once you make any changes to the specifications, fail to meet a contractual pre-arranged payment, or there is an Act of God where work has to be temporarily terminated, that initial completion date may not be enforceable.

Some contracts also include statements that spell out the procedure for supervision by the owner or foreman on the job. Management's presence on the job site will keep the work moving at an acceptable pace and cut down on repetitive work. In today's world, language barriers with workers are sensitive subjects. However, if you need something stopped or changed and you cannot be understood, it could pose problems. At the very least, you should be able to reach the contractor at all times during the project.

In all probability, in addition to the total cost of the project there will be a schedule of payments oftentimes called a draw-down. It is important for you, the home owner, to meet the agreed to terms of payment because the builder needs to pay his suppliers and workers. Failure on your part to make timely payments could cause a work stoppage and a hostile relationship may ensue.

The contract should be signed and dated by both parties. After you have carefully read the contract, signed the bottom line, and made the first payment (if required), the project is ready to start. Be sure you retain a signed copy for your records.

Have your camera ready to photograph work-in-progress from the very first day. This approach came in quite handy when I had to pursue legal remedy against a swimming pool company. That particular lawsuit went to binding *arbitration* (non-court procedure for resolving disputes using one or more neutral third parties). The photos saved the day for me; the arbitration panel was able to clearly determine who was at fault.

Over and above keeping a photo journal, it is also highly recommended that all communications with the builder be in writing. It is too easy to forget or have a misunderstanding over verbal communications. Also, a written and photographic chronology can be a tremendous aid in resolving disputes.

Very few remodeling projects with which I am familiar have gone from start to finish without an alteration to the original plan. When you deviate from the original plans, a builder refers to your instructions as a change order. This becomes an amendment to the contract. As such, it should reflect any new specifications and cost changes, then be signed and dated by both parties. Handling a change order properly will lessen additional cost disputes at the end of the job.

The final step in the process after the contractor informs you that the project is complete is for you to draft a punch list. This should identify every aspect of the project that didn't live up to your specifications and expectations, and needs to be very specific. It is suggested that you do this on your own, without the builder present. In this manner you can take as much time as you need, avoid a tangent and stay focused. Once completed, you will do a walk-through with your builder and review each item. After the builder corrects all the items on your punch list to your satisfaction, he has completed his end of the bargain and is due the remaining balance owed for the project.

Builders have leverage to insure that they will be paid. Failure to make payment may result in a *mechanic's lien* (a legal claim placed on real estate by someone who is owed money for labor, services or supplies contributed to the property for the purpose of improving it) placed on your home. Another unfortunate aspect to a mechanic's lien is that your builder's sub-contractors can also place a lien if they haven't been paid, even though your builder was paid in full. For this reason, it is highly recommended that you ask your contractor for a Contractor's Affidavit (sworn statement) that all the bills have been paid before making your final payment. This may offer you some measure of protection should you wind up in court.

With some frequency, problems do develop weeks or months after a project is complete. In some cases, product failure may be covered by a warranty. Most ethical builders will return to your property and make the necessary repairs without charge and deal with the suppliers for warranty issues. For this and other reasons, it is important to maintain good relations with your contractor throughout the process.

I must once again emphasize that choosing the right construction company with which to do business is vital.

ROOFING – Most roofing repairs arise as a result of leaks, storm damage or, to a much lesser degree, elective cosmetic changes to the appearance of your home when time is on your side for researching the right company for service.

In some instances, a new roof may be part of an overall remodeling project, in which case your builder would be responsible for sub-contracting the roofing.

Leaking and storm-damaged roofs are a different matter. Under these circumstances, you are under pressure to locate a roofer and have the work done as soon as possible. That should not preclude you from taking the proper steps to avoid getting ripped off and having to seek a resolution later.

After selecting several roofers to call, be certain to investigate each one thoroughly before contacting them. Begin with the National Roofing Contractors Association; www.angieslist.com; your local Better Business Bureau; and any other methods that will give you a level of comfort. Sometimes, an excellent roofer can be recommended by a friend who has already used his or her services. If you can, run a credit check on those companies. If you get a sense that my perception of roofers is suspect, you are correct. There are many fine, upstanding, and honest roofing contractors, but the industry also attracts scam artists and weekend warriors who are nothing more than brokers posing as substantial contractors.

The con men seem to come out of the woodwork right after a hail or wind storm hits your area. Often, they brazenly knock on your front door or leave a door hanger offering a free roof inspection. If you respond, the sales pitch will include a total job "without cost to you; not a penny." Their so-called experience and connections with the insurance companies, according to them, will enable them to waive or discount your deductible. Beware. This sales tactic is illegal in many states. If you live in a state where it is illegal and hire a firm that uses these methods, you may surrender your legal right to sue the roofer should that become necessary.

Other roofers may try to pull off the *"Elevator-Ride"* scam, where the roofer intentionally underbids the job, then finds all kinds of other phony problems. If you give them the go-ahead to fix them, you may have a legal obligation to pay, even if you discover later the work was unnecessary. Almost always those extra charges will bring the final cost above what the bid should have been in the first place. There can be legitimate hidden problems, like bad decking below the shingles and liner. A more ethical contractor will ask to walk the roof, and examine your attic and home interior for telltale signs of problems beneath the surface prior to submitting a quote.

Installing a new roof can be dangerous business due to the heights and slopes of the work environment. Thus, it is an absolute necessity that you carefully check the roofer's liability and Workers' Compensation insurance policies.

Many dishonest operators will ask for an unreasonable down payment. The accepted industry standard is one-third. Another payment may be due with the delivery of the materials to your home, which is not unreasonable. No further money should exchange hands until the job is complete and all the debris is cleared from your premises.

Learn about roofing materials before acquiring bids, which will help when negotiating the contract. Specifically, shingle prices vary widely based on quality and life-span. Some roofers will use your existing shingles as a base; others may use felt or a membrane. You can get some free advice from associates at a Home Depot or Lowes. Your computer can also be very helpful in learning more about roofing products. Due to the risks associated with putting on a new roof, the more you know the better the outcome.

LANDLORD/TENANT

In the court where I serve, lawsuits between landlords and tenants are separated by issues over damages to the property and those seeking a monetary judgment for past-due rent and/or eviction from the premises. Other jurisdictions may hear eviction cases within their civil court calendar. Regardless, the following information relates to the most common landlord/tenant disputes. Whether the property in question is an apartment, condominium, single-family house, duplex, or commercial space, the parties almost always begin their landlord/tenant relationship on an amiable basis. Typically, the landlord presents the lease; conducts a walk-through with the new tenant to examine the condition of the property; the condition report is signed; the lease is signed; a security deposit and the first month's rent are paid; and the keys are turned over to the tenant. Because there are nuances to each of these steps that can result in litigation, it is helpful to focus on them individually. (NOTE: Where references are made to "landlord," in many cases the term "Property Manager" may be substituted.)

Leases are usually drawn by the landlord or his attorney. Even though there might be an attempt to be fair to the tenant(s), leases tend to lean in the landlord's favor. Recognizing this, it is incumbent upon the tenant to carefully read every term. Handwritten modifications can be made to the lease when agreed to by all parties. Make sure that all modifications are initialed by all parties on all copies of the lease.

All valid leases should contain start and termination dates. What may become muddy are the terms if a tenant remains in the property beyond the expiration date of the lease and rents on a month-to-month basis. The debates we hear in mediation are whether the terms and conditions of the lease have been extended and are enforceable. Therefore, it is important to have a clear understanding of the lease.

All copies of all contracts should be signed by all parties. This subject will pop up throughout the Preventing section of this book, and is particularly vital in matters dealing with real estate. In many instances, verbal contracts can be binding, but as a general rule of law real estate contracts must be in writing. Verbal agreements modifying the terms of a lease will probably not hold up in court.

If a security deposit is required and the terms of the lease reference returning the property in clean, sanitary and generally the same condition as received, there should be no excuse for not doing a walk-through. The landlord should have a preprinted list of those items that may be of concern. Most inspection lists include the following:

- Overall – All doors and locks, windows, screens, HVAC system, carpets, window shades or drapes, front and back yards, all walls, all flooring, all light switches, ceilings.
- Kitchen – Stove and oven, refrigerator/freezer, sinks and faucets, cabinets and doors, counter tops.
- Bathrooms – Tub and/or shower, toilet, sink, cabinets and doors, fixtures, and mirrors.
- Bedrooms – Closets, ceiling fixtures.

If an item is not included, recovery for damages by the landlord may be difficult. Most courts do allow for normal wear and tear. The walk-through list should be signed and dated by the landlord and all those on the lease, and be easily retrievable upon termination.

The security deposit, sometimes called a damage deposit, is just that; a deposit to cover any costs incurred by the landlord to do repairs and/or extensive clean-up after the tenant vacates the premises. One month's rent is the maximum permitted in Georgia. In other states where there is a maximum, security deposits range from one-half to one-and-a-half months' rent.

Unless agreed to in writing by the landlord, the security deposit cannot be used for the last month's rent. The reason is simple: the condition of the premises cannot be determined until the tenant has removed all their personal belongings and a final inspection has been accomplished.

In Georgia, the tenant is entitled to receive his or her deposit back, minus the cost of repairs or clean-up, within thirty days after the lease has been terminated. Paid receipts for any repairs done by the landlord to bring the property to its original move-in condition should be furnished to the tenant, along with the return of the balance of the deposit minus the cost of these repairs or clean-up. If the money is not returned to the tenant in the specified period, the landlord could be responsible for TREBLE (triple) damages. This provision in the law was intended to protect the average person and may not be available for commercial leases. Conversely, if the costs of repairs exceed the deposit, the landlord has the right to collect for the difference from the former tenant. This subject is another example that can become somewhat complex from a legal perspective, and checking with a real estate attorney would be helpful.

Conflicts do arise over pets. It is in the tenant's best interest to discuss with the landlord any policies regarding pets before the lease is signed. If you own a pet, or contemplate bringing a pet into the home during the course of the lease, be sure to let the landlord know. If the lease has a no-pet policy and it is violated, the tenant can be evicted. Where pets are permitted, a separate, non-refundable pet deposit is usually required.

It is advisable for tenants to pay the first month's rent and all future rental payments by check or certified funds. When paying by cash always get a receipt. It is important for both landlords and tenants to maintain clear records of all payments. When partial payments are made it may become important later on to determine how the money was applied. While professional managers do this as a matter of course, it is the landlord with a single property who often has a problem with record-keeping. Likewise, tenants we see in mediation rarely are able to present clear rent payment records.

It is always advisable for landlords and tenants to take pictures of the property before occupancy and after they have removed all personal belongings upon termination of the lease. The photographs can be quite valuable when determining the outcome of a dispute.

The transfer of keys (and garage door remote controls, if applicable) is an exchange that can have significant impact when determining the date a tenant actually vacates the property. Even if all furniture, clothing and personal items are removed by the lease's termination date, keeping the keys can cause unnecessary problems for a tenant. A landlord who does not receive the keys at the end of the lease date may believe the tenant is still occupying the premises. For this reason, it is suggested that all keys be handed over personally, as opposed to leaving them in the mailbox or on the kitchen counter, as is often done. Tenants should request a signed and dated receipt for the keys from their landlord.

Despite complying with these recommendations, situations may arise that bring about conflict between the landlord and the tenant. Each side generally has a different view of a given situation which makes it important to understand the underlying causes if there are disputes to be resolved.

From the landlord's point of view, most conflicts begin with non-payment of rent, damage or poor upkeep of the property, or the conducting of illegal activities by the tenant. There are different remedies for each of these circumstances that may keep landlord and tenant from facing each other in court.

Unfortunately, there are times when negative financial circumstances impact the ability of tenants to pay their rent. Whether it is a good or bad economy, people still lose their jobs, get divorced, or face sudden illness that throws their budgets out of whack. The setbacks may be real, but they do not relieve the tenant of the obligation to pay the rent. When tenants focus on their own problems, they quite often forget that the landlord has mortgage payments, taxes and other costs associated with the property.

When a tenant is in dire straits, immediate communication with the landlord is the best option. Depending on the relationship between the parties and the landlord's financial ability to make concessions, an extended payment plan or other creative solutions may be possible. I have conducted mediations that have resulted in a win-win for the landlord and the tenant. But, the exchange of ideas was positive from the beginning because there was mutual respect for one another. More often than not, those parties could have resolved their differences long before coming to court, but it all starts with the tenant keeping the landlord informed.

Even when the renter faces personal adversity, he or she is still responsible for the maintenance of the property. Failure to maintain the exterior of the home, as an example, may not only be a violation of the lease, but can cause problems with the Home Owners Association and may even result in a city or county citation. Whether inside or outside, a home that is not maintained will cause conflict and difficulties when the lease expires. Friction of this nature, and potential legal costs, can be avoided simply by living up to the terms of the lease. That goes for both the tenant and landlord.

A major cause of concern by a landlord is learning of illegal activities at the property. Drug use and sales; prostitution; altercations among residents and/or their guests; violation of noise covenants; operating a business in a residential community are all examples that will cause a landlord to seek immediate eviction. As a tenant, you must cease any illegal activity. No ifs, ands or buts!

Landlords have responsibilities, too. They are required to provide structural integrity, heat (and air conditioning, if applicable); hot water; functioning bathrooms and kitchen appliances; and in some cases extermination of rodents and insects. Problems arise when these items, which are clearly the responsibility of the landlord, are neglected. In retaliation, tenants often stop paying the rent until the repairs are made. It may be a bitter pill to swallow, but it is always better for the tenant to keep up with their monthly rent payments. In my experience, courts often frown upon non-payment of rent, even under these circumstances.

Depending on the nature and timing of the breakdown, handling the situation properly will be better for both parties. There are some malfunctions that are more of an emergency than others. If it is not life threatening, take the time to contact the landlord. Discuss the options in a rational and calm manner. Certainly, no one intended or directly caused the problem. The objective for all concerned should be a reasonable and quick solution. Assuming the landlord is as concerned with the problem as you, there may be a few inconveniences you will be faced with, such as living without air conditioning for a day or two. If it is a freezing winter day and the heat is inoperable, you may have to check into a hotel until the repairs can be done, possibly at the landlord's expense. As long as measurable and acceptable progress is being made toward making the repairs, the problem is well on its way to resolution.

When problems go unresolved and the parties find themselves in court, tenants often claim they were largely ignored by the landlord and had to take action themselves. They may have been totally justified, but if they fail to communicate properly or keep receipts for monies expended they can create problems in proving their case. It is always the hope that resolution can be reached without the need for intervention.

Here are some recommendations to provide more validity to your position as a tenant:

- Communicate in writing via letter or e-mail the exact nature of the problem(s) and how you believe it should be solved. You should call the landlord as well.
- If time permits, get bids for the repair(s) and provide copies to the landlord. Give him reasonable time to respond.
- If the landlord is willing to get the repairs done in the same timely fashion as your bidders, allow him to do it, as some landlords have preferred contractors or a home warranty company. If not, in accordance with your lease, proceed with the repairs and make duplicate copies of the paid invoices. Many tenants deduct the total expenditure from the next month's rent and subsequently find themselves with a dispossession notice. To prevent that, ask your landlord, in writing, how he or she would prefer to reimburse you. Reasonable people should be able to mutually resolve this issue.

Persistent and recurring problems may legally permit you to end the lease under the law of real estate called *constructive eviction (*action or lack thereof by a landlord that compels a tenant to leave the premises). It applies if you can prove the landlord allowed the property to become uninhabitable. Another reason for upholding a constructive eviction action by a court is a landlord's intrusion into the property unannounced and without permission, shutting off utilities, or changing the locks. In addition to ending the lease you might also be entitled to damages. Before taking any formal action using constructive eviction as a basis, surf the Internet to locate a self-help web site such as: (http://definitions.uslegal.com/l/landlord-tenant-constructive-eviction/), research your state's real estate laws, or check with an attorney for guidance.

With foreclosures so prevalent, a number of suits are being heard for recovery of unpaid rent on such properties. Tenants do not realize that a landlord is entitled to collect rent until the day he or she no longer owns the property. For those tenants who wish to remain in a home after foreclosure, there are protections for them. A federal law, Protecting Tenants at Foreclosure Act (PTFA), guarantees any tenant who has a valid lease can stay, under the same terms, until the end of the lease date. However, there is an exception: if the new owner intends to occupy the home, the tenant will be given ninety days to vacate. These same conditions apply to low-income, government-supported Section 8 tenants.

Very often the new owner, usually a financial institution which would like possession sooner than ninety days, will offer "cash-for-keys," whereby the tenant can receive money as an inducement if they agree to vacate by a specified date, and leave the property broom-clean (emptied of personal property, floors cleaned, and the residence returned to the condition it was in when the lease was executed.) The amount of money usually ranges from $500 to $5,000, and depends on the terms of the lease and how quickly the tenant chooses to leave.

EMPLOYMENT

Disputes between employers and employees are a daily occurrence. Contentious issues generally fall into one of the following categories:
- An employee not being paid in a timely fashion, or not at all
- An employee not being reimbursed for legitimate expenses

- An employee stealing from employer, including money, product, time, trade secrets, or office equipment or supplies
- Inappropriate relationships with fellow employees
- Commission agreement disputes
- Wrongful termination
- Discrimination
- Harassment
- Privacy rights

Violations of any of the above can be problematic for a company or an employee if either party can prove in court that these conditions occurred. Returning to the cliché on the first page of this book, "an ounce of prevention is worth a pound of cure" is specifically and particularly true in these circumstances.

Only a small percentage of employment disputes reach a courtroom. Larger companies have Human Resource departments prepared to deal with disagreements between the company and its employees and those stemming from employee/supervisor or employee/employee problems. Many federal agencies also conduct mediation sessions for their personnel for dispute resolution.

Generally, employers in the public and private sectors want to resolve disputes internally. Yet, there are enough conflicts in the workplace to impact court calendars, so much so that most law schools offer courses in employment law.

Smaller companies often find themselves in arguments with their employees that can be avoided by establishing and following proper procedures and policies.

As an example:
- The employer should provide each employee a current company handbook, which should include an acknowledgement of receipt form signed by the employee and placed in his or her personnel file.
- The employer should follow every company policy and regulation with consistency.
- The employer should always address performance issues in a timely fashion. Allowing employee disputes

to linger can create a multitude of other problems and have a negative effect on other employees.

- When terminating an employee, the employer should communicate to the employee, in writing and with clarity, exactly why he or she is being terminated.

When personnel issues arise, most well-managed companies call for a meeting with the aggrieved employee. Because the employer is generally more experienced with these matters, sometime the employee is at a disadvantage resulting from nervousness, lack of preparation or fear of losing his or her job. To somewhat level the field, here are some hints in preparing for the meeting and suggestions on how employees should conduct themselves.

- Know your rights before going into the meeting by researching the information online. A great deal has been written and published on this topic and is easily accessible. You will find most of what you are seeking in plain and understandable language.
- In preparing for the meeting, gather all documents you are legally permitted to possess. These may include the company handbook, memos and publications that state company policy; performance reviews; all letters, emails, texts, memos and notes relating to the situation under discussion.
- During the meeting, always stick to the facts as you know them. If you are relaying what you have heard, clarify whether it was first-hand knowledge. Do not embellish or exaggerate.
- Avoid emotional outbursts; they are never productive. Realize beforehand that sensitive subjects will be discussed and react to them as best you can in a calm manner.
- Be discreet in what you say. Personal attacks never help. Placing people in the room, or those not attending, in an embarrassing position can be counterproductive. Whether the meeting is being recorded or notes are being taken, you will be responsible for what you express during the meeting.

- You may wish to take notes and keep a record of what was stated during the meeting. If the meeting did not go well, you should think carefully about your next steps.
- The only time you should consider a lawsuit is after all attempts at resolution are exhausted. Most often, suits involving discrimination, harassment or unlawful termination will be heard in a higher court than small claims court where the amount of monetary judgments are capped at a maximum $15,000 in Georgia.

Many employment cases I have handled have been over paycheck issues. In each case, there was no employment contract. The decision boiled down to whether withholding the employee's pay check was justified. It was a waste of time to be in court when a reasonable conversation between parties could have resolved the issues.

COLLECTION

The vast majority of collection cases I observe in court are between a financial institution and a debtor. Other than a loan company or collection agency, which may send its credit manager or another employee to represent them in court, virtually all the major banks and credit card companies are represented by attorneys. Other than rare circumstances where an inadvertent error took place, the attorneys almost always bring to court all the legal documentation to support their position.

The good news for the debtor, if they show up in court, is that the attorneys are generally prepared to work with the debtor to settle the case prior to going before a judge. While the parameters within which lawyers have to work is set by their clients, more often than not, a fair settlement is worked out, which might include a reduction of the debt and altering the payment plan. Not showing up in court can be a much more costly option for the debtor because as more time passes, interest charges will continue to increase.

The business of collecting money from debtors goes beyond financial institutions and credit card companies.

Plaintiffs in many lawsuits are collection agencies or loan companies. It is important to recognize that there are many honest companies seeking to recover money from borrowers. There are also unethical companies that employ questionable, if not illegal, tactics.

It is important to note that debtors do have federal and state protection from falling victim to the schemes of less-than-honorable companies. Generally, a debtor has the right to demand the collector cease calling, especially at work. The collector also is prohibited from contacting others about your debt, and the use of profanity is explicitly prohibited. A threat by the collector to have your name published in a list of debtors is also forbidden.

In many instances, the company attempting to collect is not the originator of the loan. If the signed loan documents state that, as many do, it is perfectly legal for the loan to be bought and sold. In these cases, before committing to a settlement, the borrower has the right to see the sales documents to prove ownership of the debt. Often, the loan has been bought and sold a number of times so it becomes the legal right for the borrower to examine the chain of documents. This is important so as to firmly establish that paying off the loan to the collection company will totally discharge the debtor from all claims in the future.

Once firmly established that the collection company owns the debt, the borrower should ask for, receive and carefully review the company's records of any payments that the borrower may have made, including principal, interest charges, late fees and any other charges that may have been added to the loan. Errors often occur, especially if the loan has been sold.

Based upon verification of the ownership of the loan and the amount owed, the debtor should make every effort to work out a settlement agreement with the collector. Very often the collector has the flexibility to waive fees and interest, and even agree to more favorable payout terms. In some instances, the current owner of the loan bought it for considerably less than the dollars borrowed and may be willing to negotiate the total amount of the debt. Settlement agreements can be drafted and signed before a lawsuit is filed, benefiting both parties.

HOME OWNERS ASSOCIATION

Lawsuits between Home Owners Associations (HOA) and their members appear in small claims court with regularity. More often than not, it is the HOA seeking past dues, an unpaid special assessment, or fines associated with a violation of covenants. Occasionally, a member has an unresolved financial issue with the HOA.

It is important for a new purchaser of a house or condominium, in addition to long-term rental residents, to read HOA documents and fully understand the association's By-laws and Declarations, structure of governance, covenants, and grievance procedures.

Where there is an HOA, in all probability it was established by the developer of the sub-division or condominium complex. At some point, usually after a fixed percentage of living units are sold, the developer turns over control of the association to the home owners. To assure the future viability of the association, mandatory membership by home owners is established at the outset. Each purchaser of a home, whether new or a resale, should be made aware of the HOA and its regulations in advance of the closing. If the sale of the property is being handled by a competent closing attorney or real estate broker, they will furnish the documents to the buyer on a timely basis. As a buyer, it is always advisable to inquire about HOA documents when being shown the property.

Typically, the HOA is a non-profit corporation governed by an elected board of directors who are residents of the community. The board is mandated to manage the HOA under a set of by-laws which sets the dues, conditions for special assessments, *restrictive covenants* (agreement to restrict future conduct in some manner), and other rules. These by-laws can be changed by the board, most often with the approval of the members.

In large developments, the board may choose to contract with an outside management company to collect dues and assessments, and supervise vendors such as landscapers, trash collectors, exterminators, painters, and a number of other maintenance firms. Difficulties sometimes arise because it adds another layer of decision makers when attempting to resolve a problem.

Payment schedules of HOA dues vary according to the by-laws, and can be paid on a monthly, quarterly, semi-annual or annual basis. From time to time, the board, with approval of the members, may issue a special assessment for capital improvements such as repaving. The failure of a member to meet financial obligations such as dues or special assessments can lead to fines, restrictions on the use of a clubhouse, swimming pool, tennis courts and all other amenities, as well as liens on the member's property. In extreme cases, non-payment can lead to foreclosure.

A large number of conflicts arise among members over violations of covenants which are established to maintain a high and uniform standard for the benefit of all residents of the community. **They normally cover exterior architectural changes; paint colors; yard and landscaping maintenance; use and maintenance of amenities; and parking. For those covenants that require exterior maintenance and the property properly maintained, the HOA may hire a company to do the work and charge the property owners.**

When the home owner has a dispute with the HOA, there are a number of actions that can be taken to place him or her in a stronger position to resolve the matter. If you do not have a current copy of the by-laws, get one. Search for those areas of special concern to determine if you might have a cause of action. If there is no language that covers your disagreement with the HOA, you may have an advantage.

After a careful review of the by-laws, board meeting minutes and notices that may have been sent to members, you might consider drafting a politely worded written communication to the HOA officers and property manager, if there is one. Should you mail it at the post office, send it registered, return receipt requested. Should you choose to send it via e-mail, any accompanying documents will have to be scanned as attachments. You can also fax it or hand-deliver it with all supporting documents.

The letter should state your position without accusations or demeaning language. Most importantly, offer a solution to the problem. You might also request a meeting with the board, particularly if your issue is not getting the attention you feel it deserves. When asking for a response by a certain date, keep in mind that the HOA is run by volunteers who meet on a predetermined schedule. Unless you are dealing with an emergency situation, do not expect an immediate reply.

Note that holding back dues as perceived leverage during the dispute may not be a wise decision on your part. Doing so could dramatically shift your ability to effect a change in your favor, and you might find yourself at the bad end of a legal action.

Finally, always keep in mind when trying to resolve a problem with your HOA that the officers and board members are your neighbors. They are giving their time freely to make your living environment a better place. If you are planning to remain a resident in the community, an amiable solution will not only resolve the issue at hand but will make for a better life for you and your family.

PROFESSIONAL SERVICES

There are a significant number of cases that surface in small claims court that may be generally classified as Professional Services. They include disputes with medical professionals, hospitals, and attorneys. The following information delves into some aspects that may be unique to disagreements in these areas.

MEDICAL – Quite often services are required of physicians, dentists, and chiropractors in an emergency or on an accelerated basis. Anticipating these circumstances, doctors' offices are generally set up to cover all the necessary preliminary steps, especially with new patients, to avoid the pitfalls that can subsequently lead to a dispute over billing. As a patient, it is incumbent upon you to understand, prior to treatment, the nature of services being performed and the cost of those services.

In many cases, a key component to your actual cost for medical services depends on insurance coverage. Most policies have exclusions, limitations, and co-pays that vary by insurer. In today's environment, your doctor's office personnel may be able to determine your coverage when they input your policy number. Should a procedure not be covered, you will be responsible to cover the costs.

For those without insurance or coverage for a specific procedure, the time to discuss payment is before and not after the bill arrives. If a payment plan is not acceptable to the doctor, you have the obvious choices to either cancel the procedure or find a less expensive provider. What you want to avoid is accepting services, not paying the bill, and finding yourself in a lawsuit that is difficult to defend.

Even after taking all precautions to avoid a disputed bill, it still may occur. In most cases, if you handle it properly, the doctor and his staff will cooperate with you to the extent that they can. They will want to avoid a costly and time consuming courtroom appearance as much as you do. Rather than deal with past due receivables, medical professionals will often turn your account over to a collection agency. That can lead to a most unpleasant experience for you and an additional cost for them. Therefore, working out a compromise is in the best interest of all parties concerned.

The problem of accurate billing is particularly acute with hospitals. There are hundreds of codes assigned to the myriad of procedures performed for each patient every day. These codes are posted to your chart by doctors, nurses, technicians, etc. After which the codes and related charges are kept in an electronic file until the final bill is calculated, printed and furnished to you and your insurance company or Medicare, if applicable. As soon as you receive your final bill, it should be reviewed extremely carefully. If you find any discrepancies, immediately communicate these, in writing, to the hospital's billing department. They should respond in a reasonably short period of time. If not, a follow-up email or letter from you may be necessary. Whatever their response, ask for it in writing. Hopefully, you will be able to work out the discrepancies, but if not, a paper trail may be very important to you later on.

Accident victims frequently seek the services of a chiropractor thinking that the 'at-fault' party's insurance company will pay the bill. Fees for treatment may run into the thousands of dollars and many chiropractors will delay their billing until a case is settled in court. As you will be responsible for the bill, regardless of the outcome of the case, you should have a contingency plan to pay the doctor if you lose. It is best to discuss this possibility in advance of the court hearing.

LEGAL - To understand how attorneys bill for their time and expenses, you may wish to skip to the next section of this book, where the retaining of an attorney is discussed. Misunderstandings between a client and attorney over billing issues often arises because the amount of time spent, multiplied by an hourly rate of hundreds of dollars, adds up rather quickly. Related to this is a lack of understanding by the client of what it takes to be properly represented. As a Fee Arbitrator for the State Bar of Georgia, I can also see the other side where clients were not always treated fairly or honestly by their attorneys.

Virtually every attorney who works on an hourly basis will send their client a monthly statement. Either, or both, the Fee Agreement and invoice will contain a statement requesting that the invoice be reviewed carefully and any discrepancies reported to the attorney, usually within 30 days. Having seen correspondence over the years between clients and attorneys, I can say that most attorneys will respond to a complaint about a bill quickly and in writing.

If you decide to fire your attorney, you should do so in writing. If you are firing your attorney in the middle of a case that is proceeding with another attorney or pro se, keep in mind that the first attorney can place a lien on a potential award for money owed when you terminated the relationship. Should you prevail, the first money collected would go to that attorney to satisfy the lien. From the other side the desk, there is a formal procedure for an attorney to drop a client.

Due to the strict governance over ethical conduct by attorneys and the general good character of those men and woman attracted to the field of law, most attorneys will make every effort to resolve a money dispute with a client.

In the event a dispute cannot be resolved, the State Bar of Georgia does offer a free Fee Arbitration service. (Other states may offer a similar service.) For more details, you may wish to call the State Bar of Georgia and ask for the Fee Arbitration office.

TECHNOLOGY SERVICES

There has been a fast-growing need for small- to medium-size companies to manage and market their products and services utilizing the broad field of information technology for a wide universe of business activities. Those include, among others, web site design, database development and management, distribution of products and services, inventory management, search engine optimization, personnel training, equipment installation, repair, and maintenance. The result has been an increasing amount of contract disputes that have found their way to courtrooms throughout the nation.

There are a number of common characteristics I have found in mediation conferences:
- The customer has bought a product or service that he or she does not completely understand.
- The product and related services are intangible in that the company is committing significant dollars at the beginning of a project for a product that initially cannot be seen.
- The contract is fraught with technical language.
- The customer and the provider have distinctly different personalities and technical understanding resulting in poor communications between the parties while the project is under way.
- There is often an inability by the provider to meet pre-determined deadlines.
- Technology providers are often small companies with limited time and financial constraints which can cause friction in the relationship.

- There are times when the customer fails to pay the full invoice at the end of the project.

Recognizing these difficulties in advance can help avoid conflict and insure satisfaction.

To determine what is needed and desired, management purchasing technology services should seek input from those within their organization who will be impacted. If web-site design is part of the project, for example, the comprehensiveness and the navigability by customers, suppliers, etc. must be top priorities. Researching competitor's sites can also be helpful in determining the direction of your project. The architectural detail and design of the site should be well-organized and reduced to a thoroughly vetted document, which will go a long way in producing a desirable and workable end product.

Because there are graphic design aspects, what appeals to the buyer may not match the concept of the provider. One way to mutually agree on the aesthetics is to show the tech company samples of what you like and dislike about other web sites. Flexibility and mutual trust on the part of both parties go a long way toward approval of the final design.

Obviously, a contract that cannot be fully understood by all parties is not a good way to begin a business relationship. Intrinsically, contracts for technical services contain descriptive and to some people, unintelligible language. As a result, it would be helpful to the non-technical buyer for "foreign" terms to be clearly defined. In that way, both parties are protected; the buyer knows precisely what he or she is paying for and the provider knows exactly what is expected to complete his or her end of the agreement.

In many contractual arrangements, the personalities of the parties are not significant for a successful completion. But temperaments come into play more often with technology services because of the creative, technical and communications processes. This is not to suggest that the parties go through personality changes, but to realize all three are potential sources of irritation that can lead to contractual problems. As an illustration, I had a mediation case in which the provider refused to answer telephone messages in a timely fashion because he felt the customer should log onto the work in progress and get an electronic update. This lack of communication was not only aggravating the customer, but became the beginning of a lack of confidence for the quality of the final work. My strong suggestion is to maintain regular verbal and written communications when necessary and eliminate potential conflict.

Projecting a completion date is somewhat difficult because there are many moving parts that go into a successful assignment. For the provider to keep the enterprise moving, it is incumbent upon the customer to furnish the tech company with all elements that are necessary to keep the project on schedule, such as logos, photos, copy writing, among other components. In addition, access to the client's computer system, with the necessary source codes and passwords, must be made available to the provider on an ongoing basis. Failure to do so or limiting access can have a profound impact on the projected completion date. This was actually a key factor in a mediated breach of contract dispute.

The growth in the need for technology services has created an entire cottage industry in America. By definition, the industry includes individuals, family members or friends who have formed small companies to serve the needs of the market place and who might even work from home. Most often these people are quite capable, technically, to service the needs of small- to medium-size companies.

The problem for them oftentimes is one of cash flow, making it necessary to take on additional projects because of the lack of finances. This became a major issue in a mediation case in which the customer could not supply the elements according to the pre-determined schedule, thereby forcing the provider to take on another project before completing the first one. A lack of cash flow also can create a circumstance where the provider is unable to return money demanded by an unhappy customer. An open and frank discussion regarding these conditions should be held between the parties before contracts are signed. If the customer is dissatisfied with the vendor's responses and terms, he or she should find another provider.

A large percentage of all lawsuits stem from failure to pay all or a portion of money allegedly owed to another party.

When it involves technology services, it becomes more involved, especially if there is a lawsuit filed prior to the contract being completed as a result of either the customer stopping the work or the vendor refusing to continue. Complicating matters is a determination of the value of an incomplete project. Rather than both parties losing out, which can happen in a court of law, it is always better to mediate before either party files a lawsuit.

SERVICE CONTRACTS

This heading is intended to be broad, as it represents a loosely defined grouping of cases with a common theme that are mediated at the courthouse with some degree of regularity. The commonality is rooted in the tightly written terms and conditions that extend for lengthy periods of time; some with rollover provisions. The types of companies offering these contracts include fitness centers and gyms, security and alarm companies, swimming pool service providers, landscape companies, etc. Many companies offering these long term contracts are legitimate and the contracts themselves quite legal; it's simply their method of doing business. There are others, however, who are less scrupulous and consumers must be particularly mindful when considering obligating themselves to these contractors.

The plaintiffs, for most of the cases I have seen, have been companies suing members or customers over the remaining balance due under the contract, even though their service was no longer used or desired. One such case involved an alarm company suing a customer over the two and half years remaining on the contract, even though the customer had moved, disconnected the equipment and asked to have it picked up. Another recent case involved a national fitness center chain that barred a customer from his neighborhood facility because of an argument with the manager, but refused to release him from the contract because they had another facility about twelve miles from his home that he could use. Unfortunately for the customers in both cases, they were obligated to fulfill a signed contract with stringent terms. It may be an uphill battle to have a judge rule in your favor unless you can prove that the service contracted for could not be provided or you were fraudulently induced into signing the contract.

Thus, the time to consider whether or not to take on the obligation is prior to signing. It is particularly vital to read the small print. If you don't understand any of the terms, ask for an explanation. If you disagree with any terms, discuss it with the manager of the company or facility. If privately owned, you may be able to get that term deleted by agreement. It must be scratched through and initialed by both parties on all copies, assuming that person has the authority to alter the contract. With larger companies or franchises, the management may not have the authority to alter the contract in any way. In those situations, it's take it or leave it as presented.

Always keep in mind that extended contracts presented by service companies are initially written by very competent attorneys and are often airtight. The operators know this, and will not hesitate to file suit. You may be assured that your dispute won't be their first trip to the courthouse. With a strong belief that they have the law on their side, they may not be as flexible and willing to compromise.

COHABITATION DISSOLUTION

Among the more difficult cases seen in mediation are those involving the breakup of the households of lovers, friends, roommates, or family members. Much like divorce cases, they are almost always highly emotional. A major difference, however, is that unmarried people living together do not have the protection of laws governing divorcing couples.

A constant theme that runs through these cases is they all usually begin on a friendly basis, so no thought is given to preparing a written agreement that would cover a termination of the relationship. It is difficult, if not impossible, to contemplate a separation when everything seems so perfect at the outset. Realizing that life takes unexpected twists and turns, a document should be drafted that covers the division of **personal assets**, **jointly owned property**, and **financial obligations**.

PERSONAL ASSETS – Two individuals who decide to live together generally bring with them items which have both financial and sentimental value. A document should be written that describes each item and clearly indicates ownership. If, in the future, division of these assets becomes necessary, this documentation will make the process much easier.

Whether or not an item is a gift could be a very contentious issue. An angry, emotionally distraught, or vindictive person may demand payment for or the return of items that might have been given as gifts. Copies of thank you notes, emails or text messages may help to prove the condition under which these items changed hands.

JOINTLY OWNED PROPERTY - As time progresses, people living together will make joint purchases. It could be major household items like furniture, TV's, appliances, computers, etc. A written agreement outlining disposition of these dually purchased items, in the case of a separation, should quash any arguments over ownership. The agreement should answer questions, such as whether the items in dispute should be sold and the money split or should one party buy out the other party's interest, and at what price.

It is important to note that if any of the jointly purchased items were charged to a credit card or financed by a bank or loan company, the debt holder may not allow any of the parties to be relieved of the obligation. Any nonpayment by either party will be the responsibility of both parties and will have an impact on both credit ratings. The best bet is to never cosign a note or credit card if you are not the spouse.

FINANCIAL OBLIGATIONS – Every living arrangement incurs overhead expenses ranging from rent (or mortgage payments), utilities, food, etc. Thus, it is suggested that a comprehensive budget sheet should be jointly drafted. Beside each item, the name of the person responsible for payment should be noted. If expenses are to be shared, that too should be indicated. In the event of a disagreement, this document can serve as evidence of who owes for what.

Keep in mind that a judge in many small claims courts can only award a monetary judgment for damages and will not become involved in the exchange of property or personal items. For that reason, mediation is more beneficial than a court hearing for resolving cohabitation dissolution issues. A successful mediation can result in both a monetary and property exchange resolution and an amiable parting of the ways.

Over and above the type of cases discussed previously, people do go into small claims court seeking resolution to many other conflicts arising from monetary disputes.

THE HUMAN ELEMENT

The late Rodney King posed a simple question, "Can we all get along?" Unfortunately, there is no simple answer. Human beings are complex animals with emotions, egos, and baggage full of life experiences; some good, some bad. Add to this varying levels of education or degrees of intellect, different socio-economic levels, and an array of cultural differences, and we can begin to understand why conflict is a fact of life. Our focus here is conflicts arising from doing business. However, some of the techniques presented can apply to personal disagreements with friends and family.

Volumes have been written on the human relations aspect of resolving business conflicts. Methods to work out problems prior to court trials have come to be known as Alternative Dispute Resolution (ADR). They include: *negotiation* (up and back communication between conflicting parties with the objective of attempting to find a solution); *mediation* (a procedure for bringing about agreement or reconciliation between opponents in a dispute); and *arbitration* (a procedure where the outcome is decided by an arbitrator or arbitration panel.)

According to the Oklahoma Bar Association, only five per cent of cases that are filed go to trial. That would clearly indicate that ADR procedures are being employed successfully each and every day. As we are concentrating in this section of the book on "Preventing" disputes from getting to court, mediation and arbitration will be covered in the next section, "Preparing."

Let us assume for discussion purposes that you took all the precautionary measures outlined for selecting the right company and you followed the guidelines regarding the contract. Then, subsequent to the fulfillment of the contract by one of both parties, something goes awry; as happened to my wife and me. Briefly, we added a new den to our home and during the first heavy rain water began seeping in between the outer walls. Not only were we concerned, but admittedly angry, after spending a good bit of money for what we expected would be the perfect job. I make reference to this personal situation only because of how it typifies the beginning of a dispute. It is how the dispute is initially handled that can make a major difference toward reaching a satisfactory conclusion on your own or heading down the road toward *litigation* (process of bringing and pursuing a lawsuit.)

The very first step, naturally, is to notify the other party that a problem exists. The method you use depends on the circumstances. Certainly in an emergency, like water seeping into the walls, a phone call or text is the quickest method. The benefit to a text is that a record then exists of the attempted communication. Although I prefer a detailed letter be written, an email works fine in emergency circumstances. Time permitting, certified mail or overnight delivery service where a signature is required, is preferable. Regardless of the method used, it is your approach and attitude that can impact reaching a satisfactory resolution.

It is paramount that you, the injured party, remain calm, polite and respectful. You want to avoid nastiness, profanity and accusations. There is no question that this is extremely difficult to do when you're upset. Even though the other party is absolutely at fault for causing the problem at hand, in your view, the reaction you get probably will reflect your approach. When emotions become highly charged, positioning starts to take place.

What happens next in these cases can be extremely counterproductive. The debate between you and the other party becomes a battle of wills. Ego sensitivity sets in and saving face becomes most important, and the underlying problem takes a back burner. Under these circumstances, effective communication can ultimately cease to exist and a positive outcome is rendered impossible.

Even if you say and do all the right things, you may receive an unexpected response of denial, sarcasm, and/or a raised voice. Count to ten, and allow the other party to express their frustrations, anger, hang-ups, etc. Who knows, maybe they just got bad news having nothing to do with the issue at hand. After the emotions subside, an attempt to show that you understand their point of view may go a long way toward initiating a negotiated resolution. You might even get an apology for poor conduct.

In consideration of resolution discussions moving forward amiably, a review of the current situation and possible solutions should be next on the agenda. It is always better to be flexible and consider the other side's point of view. Encourage creative solutions that will get you to where you want to be with the least damage to the other party.

It is reasonable for you to ask the other party to sign an agreement which spells out how and when the problem is to be satisfied. If they wish to draft the document, that may be acceptable, if you both have a clear understanding of all the terms to be included. Once the terms are met, hopefully the matter can be put behind you. Handled properly, even the most onerous disputes can result in preserved relationships, which may be important to both parties.

It is only when all attempts at resolution are totally exhausted that you should plan to file suit. Even then, you may try one last written communication stating your intention to do so. Include the date that you will be filing, in case the other party has a last minute change of heart and is willing to meet your terms. If you get no response by the date stated, you should move forward.

FINAL PRE-FILING CONSIDERATIONS

The process for filing a lawsuit will be discussed subsequently. However, in advance of doing so there are questions for you to answer that may require a "yes" in order to place you in the best position to win. They are not posed to give you trepidations, but represent the sobering reality of getting involved in a lawsuit.

Is your claim valid? - Being perfectly objective, and putting emotions aside, you must make a determination as to whether your case is not only valid, but provable. It may take irrefutable evidence and convincing testimony to win. If there are issues subject to interpretation, keep in mind that your opponent could have an arguable position. To assess the strength of your claim, you might wish to check with an attorney.

Are you filing in the proper jurisdiction? - Jurisdictional issues, for example, can involve either geography or dollar limitations. With regard to geography, in most cases when suing a business, either the principal location or the registered agent must be located within the county where the suit is being filed. But, there may be a contractual provision that would dictate where a suit may be filed against a company. (Like so many other facets to the law, there are other exceptions as well, such as the Long Arm Statute, which gives one state court jurisdiction over an out-of-state individual or company that caused damages locally, etc. Should questions arise in this area, you will need legal advice.)

Determining where to sue an individual is somewhat easier. The defendant must reside in the county where the suit is being filed.

Concerning dollar limitations, they may vary from state to state. At the present time in Georgia, the maximum you can sue for small claims court is $15,000. It is always advisable to check with the court clerk to determine if there have been any changes.

Is your lawsuit within the statute of limitations? - Most civil claims must be filed within a designated time frame. Also, in some states the time limitations may change depending on whether a contract in question was written or verbal. If there are any questions whatsoever about the amount of time that may have lapsed since the damages occurred and when the lawsuit is to be filed, it is important to research the matter prior to moving forward.

Are you willing to face a counterclaim? - Quite often when sued, a defendant will file a countersuit. Their counterclaim may be based on alleged damages they suffered on your behalf or for *abusive* or *frivolous litigation* (a suit without legal merit.) Even though the burden of proof switches, there is always the risk of having your case dismissed and the defendant's case affirmed. In other words, are you willing to risk paying money to your opponent that would not have been sought had you not filed the lawsuit?

Be aware that if a countersuit is for more than $15,000 (in Georgia), the case will be referred to a higher court, which will incur more expenses and require a much greater understanding of court procedures or the services on an attorney.

Is the lawsuit worth the effort financially? - Every so often cases that appear on the calendar do not make sense from a financial perspective. An example of this is a case that I had in mediation where a plaintiff was suing for $75 for the return of a deposit for services allegedly not performed. When you add the more than $100 she spent in filing fees, it made the case even more questionable. While I realize this is an extreme, there are many other cases in a similar vein.

Other financial considerations that add up quickly, in addition to the filing fee itself, are costs associated with the subpoena of witnesses, loss of pay, gas, parking, etc.

Should you choose to retain the services of an attorney, which may be advisable, the cost to litigate rises dramatically. More about that aspect of a lawsuit will be discussed in the next section.

Have you considered mediation as an alternative to filing a lawsuit? – Mediation may be an excellent method to resolve your disputed issues. A comprehensive explanation of mediation can be found on pages 89-103.

Preparing

This entire section of the book is devoted to information, plans, and actions that take place from the point at which a firm decision has been made to file suit until a conclusion is reached by a judicial order, a mediated settlement, or a dismissal of the case.

RETAINING AN ATTORNEY – YES OR NO?

The very first questions you should ask yourself are: do I need and should I retain the services of an attorney to represent me. (The same questions apply in the event a suit has been filed against you.) The answer to the first question is no. There is no requirement that a lawyer be present with you in small claims court. The second, whether you should hire a lawyer, is a much bigger decision.

There are very few absolutes presented in this book, but this is one of them. **If you can afford an attorney, and the dollar amount that you are suing for can justify the fees, the answer is an unequivocal yes.** As a non-attorney, I feel quite comfortable taking this position. Certainly, my strong endorsement cannot be considered self-serving, but is based on mediation experience and courtroom observation.

Vetting and selecting the attorney who can best represent you in your situation, is your first challenge. Every attorney is taught court procedure in law school. They learn the proper protocol. They know how to research case law. As a member of a Bar Association, they are permitted to provide representation in court. But once they graduate, like doctors, they begin to specialize. For medical care, in spite of the fact you may have an excellent internist for general medicine, if you break an arm, you will be seeing an orthopedic surgeon. Likewise, you should be seeking a litigation attorney, or at least one that spends a portion of his or her practice in the courtroom.

To get a list of prospective attorneys should not be problem. The Bar Association may have a referral service that is available to you. There are referral services and directories that you can access on your computer. Very often, litigation attorneys will locate their offices close to the courthouse. Word of mouth is another good resource. If a family member or friend felt that they were well represented by their attorney in a civil lawsuit, chances are that you too will be satisfied with your choice of the same attorney.

Many attorneys will give you a brief consultation without charge, at which time you will get a sense of his or her approach. If this person meets your criteria and also instills a level of personal comfort, you are done. If not, you may wish to interview other candidates, as a good working relationship is vital.

Mentioned earlier was the subject of affordability. How much does a lawyer cost? The answer depends on a number of factors having to do with the established basis for calculating charges and the complexity of your case. All law firms have a fee structure set by the partners and are generally based on the "going" rate for the type of legal work they do. Some lawyers work on an hourly rate basis, others on a flat fee, and still others on a *contingency fee* (funds paid as part of a favorable money award, usually a percentage) basis.

Most attorneys appearing in small claims court work on an hourly or flat fee basis. While it's not like buying a car, and shouldn't be treated as such, sometimes an attorney might be willing to negotiate a fee to some extent.

With Fee Arbitration cases I have heard at the State Bar of Georgia, and in a case that I recently mediated, I've found that disputes frequently arise for lack of an understanding of how the fees are calculated and billed. Before accepting a client, an attorney will, in all probability, present a Fee Agreement for your signature. Every one that I have seen spelled out the hourly rates, if on an hourly basis, as well as other terms and conditions. If applicable, some even detailed varying rates for senior partners, associates and paralegals.

With few exceptions, every Fee Agreement requires a *retainer* (a fee paid in advance to secure legal services.) As an illustration, if your attorney is working on a $200 per hour basis and the request is for a $1,000 retainer, you will be paying in advance for the first five hours of work on your behalf. When the five hours have expired, you may be asked for additional money as the case progresses. Some attorneys will let you pay for services rendered on an installment basis. Similarly, you may wish to find out if any part of the retainer will be refunded if your attorney spends less time on your case.

To further understand how an attorney bills for time on an hourly rate basis, the monthly invoice you receive should show a number of line items that will include the dates of services, a description of services performed and the amount of time expended for each of the individual services. If your attorney works on a ten unit per hour bases, as an example, using the $200 per hour illustration, and charges 1.5 hours for meeting with you, the cost will be $300. All the hours and all the dollars will be calculated and stated at the bottom, indicating a total amount of money owed for the time period covered by the invoice.

Keep in mind that when attorneys are billing on an hourly rate basis, it includes all the time spent on your case. Their time charges might include: face to face meetings, telephone calls, consultation with colleagues, legal research, reading and responding to letters and emails, drafting and filing *motions* (requests asking a judge to issue a ruling or order on a legal matter), and *pleadings* (written declaration of a plaintiffs allegations or a defendants responses), etc., time traveling to and from court, courtroom appearance, etc. In addition, your bill may include other expenses such as filing fees, photocopies, delivery services, etc.

Legal fees can add up quickly. There are a number of actions you can take to minimize your costs and help make the management of your case more efficient for the attorney. Prior to the first meeting with your attorney, research and organize all documents, contracts, pictures, emails, etc. that you think may be relevant to your case. When meeting with him or her, explain as succinctly as possible the entire situation; the good, bad, and the ugly. (You never want your attorney blindsided with information that surfaces well into the process.) Emails are generally better than phone calls to communicate factual information. In this manner, your attorney can read and have time to make a considered decision on the information when focused on your case. Obviously, in emergencies, or for very pertinent or timely information, a telephone call is advisable. If you can't reach your attorney personally, an associate in the office will probably be able to address your needs.

Regarding costs of representation as it relates to complexity, many cases are more cut and dry, the legal issues clear, and preparation for trial minimal. Conversely, other cases require considerable research, numerous motions to be filed, a number of witnesses to be interviewed, etc. Such cases will obviously cause charges to accumulate more rapidly.

Before moving on from the topic of fees, it must be noted that there are a number of free services available to low income people by specific legal agencies. The most prominent of these is the Legal Aid Society, whose primary function is to provide consultation and representation to people who lack the funds and the education to access the court systems in their local areas. In addition to Legal Aid, there are numerous other free legal resources available in most metropolitan communities.

Once you have a better understanding of the approximate legal costs to handle your case, you will have to make a judgment call to determine if it is worth the expenditure. If your lawsuit is for $3,500, would you be willing to spend $2,000 for fees? Probably not. But, if the suit is for $6,500, as an example, the $2,000 decision is one that you might consider. Only you can make that decision.

Before making a final decision, the following are a number of considerations in favor of retaining an attorney:

Assess quality of your position – Soon after listening to your position and examining the evidence in your possession, your attorney may be able to determine your chances of prevailing in court. They will detach the emotions and focus on the facts, as he or she sees them based upon the legal argument that will have to be made in court. It could be that your case is without merit, and it is far less expensive and stressful to find out early in the process. Conversely, you may find that you have a strong case, which is no guarantee of success, but perhaps more assuring.

Lawyer's letter – Even though you believe that every avenue toward settlement has closed, a single demand letter to your opponent from your attorney will clearly indicate the seriousness of the matter and your intent, and may result in moving him off dead center. As late as it may seem, you may still have the opportunity to avoid a lawsuit.

Complicated system – We live under the greatest legal system in the world, but it is fraught with confusing twists and turns. It is extremely difficult for a layperson to properly research case law that may be germane to the issue at hand. Litigation attorneys do this for a living. Also, with their broad trial experience, they may have had similar cases, thereby allowing them to quickly pinpoint the supporting legal arguments that can win the case for you. I have seen pro se parties try to present case law that they have researched, only to have it struck down by the judge due to misinterpretation of the law or its relevance.

Filing properly – Most magistrate courts make it as easy as possible for the general public to file suits on their own (as we will be discussing later). However, a properly and timely filed case can be assured when handled by an attorney. An improper filing can delay a case or possibly cause it to be dismissed. Additionally, there may be motions to be filed, subpoenas to be issued, and other supporting legal documentation for your case which you may not know how to prepare and present.

Courtroom decorum – Attorneys know how to act in front of a judge; when and when not to speak. They know when to make an objection. They know how to prepare and to present evidence. They know how to challenge or ask to suppress an opponent's evidence. All these attributes can go a long way toward a favorable decision.

Ally at your side – For most people that I have observed, appearing in court is a nerve wracking experience. Having your attorney with you is a calming factor. You will undoubtedly hear things that you don't like, or believe to be lies. A natural reaction on your part would be to show temperament vocally or through body language, which judges will not accept. Your attorney can keep that from happening.

Prepping witnesses – Your attorney can review the testimony of your witnesses in advance and give guidance as to their presentation. Also, if your opponent has witnesses, your attorney can *Invoke the Rule* of sequestration (make a request that a witness be prevented from hearing other witnesses during a trial.)

Opponent brings attorney – It could be that you show up in court pro se and the other party is being represented by their lawyer. As strong as your case appears to you, this may make winning somewhat more difficult when your testimony or evidence is being professionally challenged by an opposing attorney. Conversely, it may be to your advantage to be represented when the other party is not.

Potential of a countersuit – Often, when sued, the other party will file a *countersuit* (a claim made by a defendant against a plaintiff in a legal action) with their answer. Whether you feel it has merit or not, it will have to be addressed at trial (or in a settlement discussion.) An attorney at your side can place you in a better position to address countersuit issues in the courtroom.

Art of negotiation – The law requires that a good faith effort be made to resolving a lawsuit before trial. Who might be better at negotiating a reasonable settlement: a professional, who does this for a living, or you?

If you lose – As hard as your attorney has worked preparing and presenting your case, it is entirely possibly that you could be ruled against. Some cases may still have merit and can be appealed to a higher court. An attorney can make a proper assessment of your chances on appeal and make a recommendation, one way or another. He or she will also have the advantage of hearing firsthand how the opposing party presented their case during the small claims trial. The filing of the appeal would also be handled by your attorney, in a proper and timely fashion.

***

The American Bar Association, in 1991, conducted a survey to determine why parties to a lawsuit elect to represent themselves in court. The result of their research indicated that there are five primary reasons: 1) lawyers were too expensive, 2) lawyers did not deliver quality services, 3) the case was simple enough to handle themselves, 4) people felt that they knew their situations best, and 5) people wanted to be in control of their own lives. While the study didn't cite percentages, the majority contested of cases I have seen in small claims court have been with the parties representing themselves. Therefore, the next phase will address filing a lawsuit on your own in small claims court.

PRE-FILING TASKS

Even people with the calmest demeanor can have anxiety issues when contemplating the filing of the lawsuit. For certain, it is a decision that requires much thought and it's likely that the disputed issues have dominated your mind for quite a while. For that reason, there are a number of suggestions you might consider to help reduce tension and enhance your chances of success.

Initially, you may wish to create a logically sequenced "to do" list, including: gathering *evidence* (documents or testimony presented in court to prove a truth or falsity); contacting potential witnesses, and planning a strategy.

The **evidence** to be assembled might include contracts, amendments to contracts, paid receipts of costs associated with damages, related bank accounts, cancelled checks, business records, time sheets, correspondence (letters, emails, texts), recorded conversations, manufacturer's published material, warranties, guarantees, photographs, etc. (If estimates are to be used as evidence, the court may require the person preparing the estimates to appear in court as a witness.)

Photographs can play a significant role as evidence when illustrating damages or the present condition of property. If you are planning to use photographs as evidence, how they are taken, processed, and marked should be carefully considered. It is a safer bet to plan on using prints as opposed to images on a smart phone. Some judges will refuse to accept as evidence any item shown on an electronic device. For those who will, a large tablet may be best to show the actual damage.

With regard to print size, the larger the image the better. For example, an 8 x 10 is better than a 4 x 6. Litigants often use photocopy reproductions as evidence where poor clarity can become an issue. Whichever you choose to use, write a brief description of the subject matter on the back of the photograph. It would also be helpful to know the date the photo was taken and the photographer's name. As with your other evidence, all photos should be numbered in the same sequence as the written evidence.

Once satisfied that you have all the evidence in hand, it is important that you carefully reread all the written material and review your photographs. It might be helpful to make photocopies of your documents and mark the applicable points with a highlighter. This can help you organize your testimony.

In determining who may best support your position, a list of potential witnesses should be developed. These people should have direct, first-hand knowledge of the facts or be experts in their respective fields. In most cases, you may wish to interview these people to make a determination as to what they actually know about the facts of the case and ascertain whether or not they are willing to testify on your behalf. For expert witnesses, it may be necessary to negotiate with them a fee for appearing in court.

After completing these tasks, the next step is for you to develop a **strategy**. At trial, you will be giving oral testimony, presenting evidence, introducing your witnesses, cross examining your opponent's witnesses, answering questions from the judge and/or your opponent (or his or her attorney), and possibly making a closing statement. It is absolutely essential that you present a well thought out, comprehensive, yet compact, presentation. Being well organized and succinct is especially important when you are "on the clock", based on the time allotted to you as per your request. Judges in small claims court are patient, but they do not appreciate fumbling around and searching through disorganized evidence.

If you have watched attorneys at work in a courtroom, you will notice that they continually refer to their notes. Therefore, it is highly suggested that you too outline your testimony, from beginning to end, on a pad.

Your notes should be aligned with your testimony, documents and photographs. Each piece of evidence to be handed over to the judge should be marked sequentially P-1, P-2, P-3, etc. if you are the plaintiff (and D-1, D-2, D-3, if you are the defendant).

Without putting words in their mouths or influencing their testimony, you should have a clear understanding of what your witnesses will be telling the judge. The judge usually does not want to hear cumulative testimony, a repeat of what you, or another witness, has already stated.

You may also anticipate that you, and your witnesses, will be *cross examined* (questioning of a witness by an opposing party). If you have any idea of what may be asked, a thoughtfully preplanned answer might be helpful. Likewise, you might wish to develop a set of questions for your opponent in anticipation of what they will be likely to say before the judge.

If you are planning to make a closing statement, it will be your opportunity to summarize your position and convince the judge that a ruling should be handed down in your favor. You may wish to write it out verbatim. The judge will not mind if you read it. The key is to be brief and to the point.

Due to the importance of evidence in all court cases, the following two final suggestions are made to avoid the potential adverse effect on parties who do not comply.

- **Bring all your evidence to court.** I hear repeatedly by one party or the other in mediation that evidence exists, but was forgotten or deemed unimportant. After realizing the significance of this evidence, they often ask for time to retrieve it; a virtual impossibility when their case is about to be heard.

- **Submit your evidence to the judge.** It is not the judge's job to ask for any evidence to support your case. As a result of nervousness or carelessness, I have seen parties fail to present evidence in their possession during mediation that could have changed the outcome of their case.

FILING PROCEDURE

The manner in which the filing forms are filled out can have a major impact on your case. Most courts have web-sites. After locating the page related to your need, it is always best to follow the directions explicitly when filing or answering a lawsuit. Rather than file or answer incorrectly, a telephone call or personal visit to the courthouse may be helpful. For those unable to use or access a computer, paper instructions and forms are also available for distribution at the courthouse.

Once you have met all the criteria for filing suit against the right parties, in the right jurisdiction, other considerations are: the accuracy of the information you provide; the justification for the money damages sought; and the question of subpoenas.

Very close attention should be paid to the names of those being sued. For individuals, you'll want to be sure that you are using your opponent's full legal name. This is also true for their complete address; particularly for service reasons. For businesses, you will need the exact legal name of the company, as registered with the Secretary of State's office. You may wish to match that name with any invoices or letters that you have received from the company to be sure there are no discrepancies. The last thing you will want to happen is to show up in court and have the case dismissed due to the wrong party or company being sued. It happens on a regular basis.

Determining how much money to sue for is also a major component to your filing papers. Other than the possibility of accruing interest (under a contract), or the potential of recovering legal fees, it is highly unlikely you will receive any more money than the damages claimed when filing.

Regardless of the amount, it will be your burden as plaintiff to prove the liability of the defendant and the exact damages supported by your evidence. When parties start adding unsubstantiated dollar amounts to the lawsuit for things like repayment for one's own labor, stress, disrespect, etc., they begin to lose credibility and potentially weaken their case. Plaintiffs often seek compensation for "pain and suffering." Generally, in order for a judge to consider an award on that basis, there must have been physical impact to one's person. In the final analysis, you may ask for any amount you care to within the jurisdictional limit of the court, but be ready to provide proof.

Lining up and interviewing witnesses should take place before you actually file. If it's questionable whether or not significant witnesses to your case may actually show up in court, you have the option to subpoena them. To do so, however, you will incur additional costs. Also, you'll want to be absolutely sure of the proper home and work addresses so that the person can be properly served the first time, whether by the sheriff or private process server.

The following information is provided to give you a general idea of how the filing process works, though it may be somewhat different in your local jurisdiction.

To file a lawsuit, the very first action is taken by the plaintiff, either through a visit to the courthouse or online. A Statement of Claim must be completed. The form requires the names, addresses, and phone numbers of all those filing the suit and all those being sued. Space will be allotted for the plaintiff to describe in detail, in his or her own words, why the defendant is indebted to them. In addition, there will be space to indicate how much you are suing for as well as the amount of court costs. Just above the signature line will be a statement attesting to the truth of the claim against the defendant.

Once you, as the plaintiff, are satisfied that the Statement of Claim is totally accurate, you will submit it to the clerk's office, along with payment of the filing fee. Some jurisdictions will only accept cash, money orders, or major credit cards from individuals. Businesses, however, may pay by check. A portion of the filing fee is used to pay for *service* (notification to the other side that a lawsuit has been filed) by the sheriff's office. This part of the fee may increase with each defendant. The total amount of fees may vary, depending on the jurisdiction. Most counties do have provisions for fee waivers based on certain criteria for those who cannot afford to pay. The party seeking a waiver may be asked to sign a *Pauper's Affidavit* (sworn statement by a party that they are unable to pay a filing fee).

After the lawsuit has been filed, the defendants will be served with a copy of the complaint and a summons. Every state and court has specific times in which to answer. It is advisable to check with your local court to determine the required time frame. The consequences of not answering or answering late can be very damaging.

If there is to be a counterclaim, it is usually included within the defendant's answer when filed, depending on the rules of your local court. Even though the dollar amount of a plaintiff's claim is within the limits of the small claims court, if the amount of the counterclaim is in excess of that limitation, the case could be sent to a higher court.

If you have any questions about the filing procedure, the clerk's office will be happy to assist you. They cannot give you legal advice, but can help with the forms and answer procedural questions.

It is extremely important for the clerk's office to be kept informed of any address or telephone number changes for you and your witnesses during the entire course of the proceedings.

Having completed the filing process, the following information deals with aspects of the trial.

COURT DAY

Both parties to a lawsuit, plaintiffs and defendants, plus their attorneys, will receive by mail a notice to appear. It will indicate a case number, date and time to appear, the address of the courthouse, and the assigned courtroom.

It is imperative that you are present in court by the designated time. Failure to appear by one or both parties can result in a dismissal of the case or a judgment against the party who failed to appear. Therefore, in consideration of every day commuting problems, such as traffic, mechanical breakdowns, traffic accidents, parking availability, etc., it would be my suggestion that you leave quite a bit earlier than you would for a routine appointment.

The issue of parking may seem insignificant in the total context of your day in court. But it can be quite important if the courthouse where your case is to be heard doesn't have ample parking near-by. Those in largely urban settings are more problematic for the general public. There are three concerns related to this issue: distance, costs, and length of time permitted.

Simply put, the further away you may have to park, the more time it will take to get to the courthouse. Some lots will charge by the hour and others by the day. Still others may allow you to park for a maximum of two hours. As for the latter, you may not be able to leave the courtroom to move your car, which can create other problems. Many people file and respond on-line and may not be familiar with the area surrounding the courthouse, so it might be worthwhile to drive to the area and learn in advance what the parking situation is like. Even more advantageous would be a visit in advance to the courthouse in order to locate the courtroom to which your case has been assigned.

Furthermore, once you have arrived at the courthouse, consider that it will take additional time to pass through security and locate the courtroom. It's a much safer bet to show up early than not being in the courtroom when your name is called.

It is always advisable to have the court clerk's phone number in the event of an extreme emergency. A continuance may be possible under special circumstances, such as a medical emergency or the death of a family member. You may be asked, subsequently, to provide convincing evidence of the reasons that caused your non-appearance.

COURTROOM SETTING

A number of people tell us in mediation that prior to their case, they had never been inside a courtroom. So to familiarize readers with similar inexperience, the following is a description of the courtroom itself and what can be expected upon entering.

The basic layout of an American courtroom is fairly standardized. As you enter the main doors, usually at the rear, take note that the room is divided in two sections, separated by a low barrier, sometimes referred to as the "bar."

The section you enter is called the gallery and is most often furnished with pew style benches. In small claims court, this is the area designated for the parties to a suit, their witnesses, attorneys, and the general public.

Just beyond the barrier is the area where all matters before the court will be handled. The two tables nearest this divider are called counsel tables. These tables are placed there for use by the attorneys and their clients. Just in front of these tables is an open area referred to as the well. Most often, the parties will be asked to stand in the well, before the judge, to give their testimony.

On one side of the well there may be chairs along one wall for the bailiff and other court personnel. On the reverse side, there may be a jury box. Even though small claims cases are not jury trials, many court rooms serve multiple purposes and are therefore designed with a jury box.

Facing the well is the workspace for the court clerk. To the side of the court clerk's desk there is another space that is for the use of a court reporter. In small claims cases, if a court reporter is present, they would have been hired by one or both of the parties, not provided by the county.

The elevated area just beyond the court clerk's desk is the judge's workspace, known as the bench. To the judge's side, there will be an area designated as the witness box.

Other than the main doors where the public enters, there are side and rear doors that are for use by authorized personnel only. The judge will enter from a door directly behind the bench.

COURTROOM PERSONNEL

In addition to the previously described courtroom layout, it is also important to learn who comprises the courtroom personnel and have a general understanding of their respective duties during a hearing.

JUDGE:
- Reads documents on pleadings and motions to ascertain facts and issues.
- Rules on motions
- Presides over hearings and listens to allegations made by the parties to determine whether evidence supports claim (or counterclaim, if filed).
- Rules on admissibility of evidence and methods of conducting testimony.
- Asks parties questions regarding testimony and evidence submitted
- Monitors proceedings to ensure that all applicable rules and procedures are followed within laws of the jurisdiction.
- Ensures that all witnesses and attorneys keep arguments and testimonies to the point
- Rules on objections
- Advises litigants, attorneys, and court personnel regarding conduct, issues and proceedings.
- Writes decisions on cases.
- Awards judgment to prevailing party or takes case under advisement for a later decision.

COURT CLERK:
- Serves as administrative assistant to the judge.
- Performs clerical duties in court.
- Administers the oath to witnesses.

- Assists in the administration of the court to insure it runs smoothly.
- Records case dispositions and court orders.

BAILIFF:
- Checks the courtroom for supplies and cleanliness.
- Opens court by announcing the arrival of the judge.
- Enforces courtroom rules of conduct and warns all in attendance not to disturb court proceedings.
- Maintains order in the courtroom during a trial.
- Delivers court documents to the parties.
- Closes court by announcing the judge's departure.

DEPUTY:
- Responsible for the safety of the judge, courtroom personnel, and visitors
- Arrests any party with an outstanding warrant
- Arrests any party, by order of the judge, on a *contempt* (deliberate disobedience of the rules, orders, and/or policies of a court) citation.

There are other people associated with the operation of the courtroom that may be present during your day in court.

ALTERNATIVE DISPUTE RESOLUTION SUPERVISOR (MEDIATION COORDINATOR):
- Assigns cases to mediators.
- Answers questions by mediators during a mediation conference.
- Assists mediators with preparation of settlement documents.
- Secures judge's signature for settlement documents.
- Distributes copies of settlement documents to mediator.

MEDIATORS:
- Escorts parties from courtroom to mediation conference rooms.

- Reviews guidelines for mediation with the parties.
- Conducts mediation sessions.
- Assists parties in the preparation of settlement documents.
- Secures signature of the parties on final settlement documents.
- Distributes final settlement documents to the parties.

COURT REPORTER:
- Takes down verbatim rendition of the proceedings.
- Creates an accurate written transcript.
- Certifies authenticity of written transcripts.
- If applicable, provides the deaf and hard of hearing with closed caption and real time translating facilities.

COURT INTERPRETER (TRANSLATOR):
- Translates from a foreign language to English verbatim what is said by the parties, the judge, the attorneys, and the witnesses during a court proceeding. Appointment often required.

COURTROOM DECORUM

To a large extent, rulings by the judge in a small claims court are influenced by the credibility and demeanor of the parties, and especially so where there is no written contract. Additionally, some written contracts are fairly ambiguous, and are thus subject to interpretation. In any of these situations, the conduct of the litigants can have a bearing on the decision that is handed down. Taking this notion a step further, regardless of the strength of your legal position, **the dignity of the Court must be respected and maintained at all times**. The following describes two essential aspects of courtroom decorum: **attire** and **conduct**.

ATTIRE - One word captures the essence of how you should dress for court: appropriately. Many courts publish acceptable dress codes specifying articles of clothing that are unacceptable, such as: miniskirts, tank tops, cut offs, midriff tops, visible undergarments, etc. It is also advisable to avoid provocative dress, T- shirts with cute sayings, and torn or dirty clothes. You may also be asked to remove hats and dark glasses.

On the other hand, it is never necessary for men to wear a coat and tie or women to wear a fancy dress. Conservative and clean should be your guideline. As many litigants will be returning to work directly from court, wearing their work uniform is perfectly acceptable, too.

CONDUCT - Court cases may not be won on good behavior, but can be lost by poor behavior. In all courts there is an expected level of conduct to be maintained. As this book is being written primarily for the less informed, I will document reasonably anticipated conduct from the moment one steps into the courtroom, through the trial itself, and beyond. Listed are expectations for pre-trial and trial conduct:

PRE-TRIAL

Prior to the calendar being called the gallery will begin to be occupied by the parties to the proceedings and visitors. As a participant, it is important for you to be aware of those rules governing the court in advance of your appearance.

CELLPHONES AND PAGERS – Should your phone or pager interrupt a court proceeding, it may be confiscated by the deputy. Thus, not only should the ringer be shut off, it is suggested that the vibration mode also be in the off position. If you are unsure how to accomplish this task, you might wish to remove the battery.

FOOD AND DRINK – Dump all your food and drink in a trash receptacle prior to stepping into a courtroom. It would be best to do the same with chewing gum and tobacco.

SEATING – Unless the calendar is extremely full, there will be a seat for everyone in the gallery. Should standing become necessary for lack of space for seating, the bailiff or deputy will issue instructions on where to stand. The main doors are to be kept clear at all times.

QUIET - It is expected that you will refrain from all conversation when being addressed by the judge or other court personnel during court proceedings. Should you have any need to speak to others, it would be best to do it outside the courtroom.

CHILDREN – Courts do not provide childcare. It is always best to leave all small children at home. If that is not possible, be sure to have someone with you to take them out of the courtroom should they create a disturbance.

HEARING IMPAIRED – You should let the bailiff know when you enter the courtroom if you are hard of hearing. In this manner, the court will be informed when the calendar is called and during the trial.

RESTROOM BREAK - Should you need to use the restroom just prior to the call of the calendar or your case is being called, it may be advisable to tell the Bailiff.

COURT IN SESSION

At the precise time designated for the court to be in session, and after the parties are sworn in, the Bailiff will ask everyone to rise as the judge enters. The judge will then greet those assembled in the courtroom.

Opening remarks from the judge may vary from a brief welcome and a request for the parties to a *contested case* (an action which involves disputes between parties on facts or law) to leave the courtroom and make for one last attempt to settle the dispute, to a comprehensive overview of what is to follow. As it is important, in my view, for you to clearly understand the ensuing procedure, the following is a step-by-step walk-through of a more comprehensive overview given by some judges.

Most judges will announce first their names, identify themselves as presiding judge, and then state the jurisdiction represented by their court. You may next hear an explanation of the types of cases on the day's calendar. In small claims court, they will typically be described as: cases over **pending motions**; **default hearings**; and **contested civil matters**.

They can be defined as follows:

Pending Motions – For these cases, the judges will hear issues of motions and make a ruling. As an example, these may be: motions to *compel* (asking the court for an order to force the opposing party to produce documents); motions for a *continuance* (postponement of a court case for a future day); or motions pertaining to issues regarding the proper parties to a suit or the proper jurisdiction, etc.

Default Hearings – These are cases where the defendant failed to answer the suit in a timely fashion or didn't show up in court after being served, and the plaintiff is asking for a favorable ruling. The plaintiff must then be prepared to demonstrate evidence of damages. Successfully accomplished, a judgment, in all probability, will be issued in their favor.

Contested Civil Matters – These are cases in which the plaintiff files a complaint for damages that is opposed by the defendant. A defendant may deny the claim, and when a counterclaim has been filed, both allegations will be heard consecutively.

The next topic the judge may cover deals with the burden of proof. In all American civil courts, the burden of proof rests with the plaintiff. In small claims court, this burden is lower than that of criminal courts, where "beyond reasonable doubt" is necessary to prove one's case. The lower standard can be described as a *preponderance of the evidence* (more likely than not.) A visual example of this might be a scale on which the weight of one's evidence must tip the scale in their favor.

Next, the judge may give an explanation of what constitutes hearsay evidence. As the rules governing hearsay evidence are quite extensive and vary a great deal from state to state, and are subject to change, most discussions on the topic that I have heard deal with two just facets, one having to do with certain types of documents and the other with testimony regarding a third party. As evidence is so vital to proving one's case, it is important to be sure that what you bring to court will be considered valid. In the same light, making arrangements with the preparers of your evidentiary documents and expert witnesses to appear in court to support your case is a major decision you have to make.

Generally speaking, estimates to do repairs, police reports, written communications from third parties etc., may not be acceptable or might carry less weight with the judge unless the preparer of those documents is in court. Also, the opposing side may object to the submission of the evidence if they cannot cross examine the preparer.

Hearsay testimony would be a statement made in court by one party repeating what was heard from a third party not in court. As an example, statements like "my brother Joe told me this" or "the man at the repair shop said..." are considered hearsay. If the parties making the statements are not in court, testimony on their behalf will not be accepted by the judge.

Many judges will then speak about the requirements for the litigants in a civil contested case to step out of the courtroom and make a good faith effort to settle the dispute before coming to trial and to share all evidence with the opposing party. If a piece of evidence is withheld from the other party, the judge could refuse to accept it.

Should the parties reach an agreement prior to the trial, there are pre-printed forms made available by most courts to memorialize the terms of the agreement. If the agreement is more complicated, a member of the court's Alternative Dispute Resolution staff can provide the assistance you may need to draft the final document. Once signed by all parties, notify the bailiff or the court clerk and he or she will arrange to have it read and, if the terms are within the boundaries of the case, presumably signed by the judge.

To help facilitate the resolution of disputes, many small claims courts will offer the assistance of a mediator. In many jurisdictions the service is provided free to the parties by the county. Some courts will have mediators and conference rooms available on-site, so that mediation conferences can begin immediately after agreement by the parties. Other courts require arranging mediation by appointment. (A full discussion of mediation will follow the information about the calendar call.)

CALENDAR CALL

Immediately following opening remarks, the judge will begin the calendar call. The calendar itself is a computer generated list of all cases to be heard during the session. Information on this list includes: sequential position numbers; case numbers; names of all litigants and their attorneys, if represented.

Beginning at the top, one case at a time, the plaintiff's name is called first, followed by the defendant's. There is a requirement in all courts that you **only answer for yourself during the call of the calendar**. As an example, you are not allowed to respond for your spouse, who might be parking the car. Attorneys will generally answer the call by stating their name and saying whether they are representing the plaintiff or defendant. For companies, only owner(s), full-time employees, or an attorney can respond.

Should the plaintiff appear, but the defendant does not, a judgment will be issued for the plaintiff, if the defendant admitted to the claim in their answer. However, where the claim was denied, the plaintiff will have to present evidence to the judge proving the amount of damages before the judgment is awarded. On the other hand, if the defendant appears, but the plaintiff does not (or neither party appears), the case will generally be dismissed for *want of prosecution* (failure of a party to appear for trial).

One circumstance that surfaces quite often is when an attorney submits a conflict letter or notifies the court by phone, in advance, that he or she has been scheduled to appear in another court at the same time. In those instances, the judge may allow a continuance. The same might be true if the clerk was notified by one of the parties of a medical emergency, death of a family member, or some other acceptable reason as determined by the judge. Often, only one continuance will be allowed.

Assuming all parties to the lawsuit respond when their name is called, the judge may ask how many witnesses each side has, including themselves, and to estimate the length of time required by each side to plead their case, including cross examination of the opponent. In most of the civil cases that I have seen, the parties will request between five and 15 minutes per side. It is important to give an accurate estimate of time, as most judges will hold the parties to it.

In the court where I serve, the judge will next explain and offer the option of mediation. In order to move forward with mediation, both parties have to agree. Although, a judge can order mediation. Those mediating will be escorted from the courtroom to a nearby conference room.

MEDIATION

Most litigants in small claims actions will be offered the opportunity to jointly reach an agreement through mediation, and thus avoid the risks associated with a trial. The following information is intended to fully explain what mediation is, the many benefits, how it works, and what can be expected as a result of a successful or failed conclusion.

BACKGROUND

Even though the practice can be traced back to its development in ancient Greece, we now find mediation gaining in current prominence within our legal system since implementation by the United States Department of Justice in 1977. However, most people are not familiar with its application in their own environment.

By way of definition, mediation is **"a process for bringing about agreement or reconciliation between opponents in a dispute."** Although often confused with "arbitration", there are clear differences. Arbitration is a quasi-formal procedure where the outcome is decided by the arbitrator or arbitration panel, as the case may be. Parties are sworn-in and the rules of evidence apply, much like that of a trial in the courtroom setting. Decisions in arbitration can be legally binding and overturned on appeal.

Contrast this to mediation, where the parties themselves determine the outcome. The role of the mediator, as a totally neutral party, is to assist the parties in conflict to develop a mutual understanding of the issues and work toward building a practical, acceptable, and enduring resolution.

BENEFITS

Control one's destiny – Perhaps the biggest single benefit to mediation is that both sides to a dispute have the ability to decide their fate. The alternative is to have a judge, in a matter of minutes, make a decision, which will definitely make one party and sometimes both, very unhappy. I have sometimes been surprised when a judge's decision proved to be the exact opposite of what might have been expected.

More "tools" available - In many small claims court jurisdictions, the judge can only award a judgment for a lump sum dollar amount to the prevailing party. A mediated agreement can be forward looking and far more flexible. As an example, payment plans can be formulated to resolve the money issues. Or, by mutual agreement, the case can be continued until work is performed to complete a contract. An example of this may be where a homeowner withholds the final payment to a painter because of dissatisfaction with the job. Arrangements can be made, in writing, for the painter to redo that portion of the work that caused dissatisfaction, and upon completion, get paid. Another example might be an agreement where the exchange of property would satisfy a claim. Both arrangements can be resolved through mediation.

Save time (and money) – Due to the lengthy calendars in many courts, the litigants and their witnesses must remain in the vicinity of the courtroom for hours waiting for their case to be called. This may mean loss of additional wages, higher attorney fees, and increased expenses for parking, etc. My experience has been that a typical small claims mediation session generally will not exceed one hour. Once all the documents are signed, the parties are free to leave without returning to the courtroom.

Assistance with documentation – A successful mediation will result with a *Consent Judgment* (a final judgment of the court based on an agreement between the parties to settle the matter and end litigation), a *Consent Agreement* (a voluntary agreement between two legal parties to solve a dispute in a court action), *Consent Order* (an order of the court which has been entered into voluntarily by the parties to a lawsuit), a dismissal, or a combination, depending on the terms and conditions. A mediator is trained to assist the parties in drafting the appropriate documents that may have been customized to the needs of the parties. If the documents require the judge's signature, it can be facilitated by the mediator.

Increased chance of compliance – When parties voluntarily come to an agreement, there is a greater tendency to comply with the terms. Conversely, an order of the court may be resisted by the losing party in every way possible.

"Dress rehearsal" - Participating in mediation is rarely a waste of time. Even when no settlement is reached and the result is an impasse, the parties are considerably better prepared for trial. There are a number of reasons for this.

The oral presentation made during an opening statement in mediation is very similar, if not the mirror image, of what you will be telling the judge. Due to the more relaxed atmosphere, it becomes your opportunity to practice without fear of misstating facts, getting lost in your own words, or omitting pertinent information due to nervousness. You may even find the time to make additions, deletions, or corrections to your presentation between the termination of the mediation and the start of your trial.

Organize evidence – One significant requirement for pre-trial is to exchange evidence with your opponent. In mediation, perhaps through questioning by the mediator, you will be organizing your evidence in the same logical sequence that is helpful for presentation before the judge.

Preview opponent's presentation – Each side will be able to hear their opponent's argument in advance of trial. This may enable you develop questions that you may use to weaken their testimony and evidence during cross examination.

Reduce anxiety – Most people are somewhat anxious when they have to appear before a judge. Very often appearing as a litigant in court is a new experience. There may be a considerable sum of money at risk. And, you may be confronting an individual who makes you feel uncomfortable. Whichever the case, a mediation conference can take the edge off and allow you to enter the courtroom in a more confident and positive frame of mind.

****

FORMAT

The format employed in civil mediation is fairly standard. Once everyone is gathered in a conference room, the mediator will introduce him or herself and then check the case file to be sure that all named parties to the lawsuit are present. There are two schools of thought as to who else, other than the named parties, may attend a mediation session. As a general rule, with permission of the opposing party, I will allow family members and/or witnesses to be present. I find that the moral support and additional information that they can provide can be helpful. In addition, to deny permission can often add to the tension. Other mediators, however, feel that non-named parties can be a hindrance, will not allow them to be present. From experience, I can say that it works both ways.

Prior to beginning the actual mediation, virtually all jurisdictions require that their "Guidelines" be read and signed by all participants. I make a point of reading the guidelines to the assembled group to be sure that they are fully understood and to take the opportunity to make editorial comments that I feel will be helpful toward a successful outcome for the mediation. Due to the significance of this document, and the fact that a number of questions about the mediation process can be answered, I am including the exact wording used for the Guidelines in the

Magistrate Court of Cobb County Georgia. (The language used in this set of guidelines is very similar to that used in a number of other jurisdictions in this area.) There will be personal notations (*in italics*) that I regularly state during a mediation conference for the benefit of the parties or for informational purposes related to the matter at hand.

GUIDELINES

Mediation is a process by which a Neutral facilitates settlement discussions between the parties. The Neutral has no authority to make a decision or impose a settlement upon the parties. The Neutral attempts to focus the attention of the parties upon their needs and interests rather than rights and positions. In the absence of the settlement, the parties are still eligible to appear before a judge to plead their case.

("Neutral" is just another name for a mediator. With regard to settlement, it is noteworthy that approximately 70% of cases are settled in mediation in the court with which I am associated.)

By signing below, the parties understand that:

1. Information gathered in the mediation process is confidential and privileged. Neither the mediator nor any court designee shall willingly testify for or against either party involved should either party end the mediation process and litigate the matter in court.

    (Confidentiality is universally required in all mediations. The only exceptions in civil mediations are threats to self, others in the room or when the safety of a third party is jeopardized.)

2. Both parties are expected to negotiate in an atmosphere of good faith and full disclosure of matters material to any agreement being reached.

(It is the law, in Georgia, that negotiations take place, with or without a mediator. However, there is a greater chance of reaching a settlement and avoid going to trial when a mediation conference is held.)

3. The mediator is not acting in the capacity of an attorney or financial advisor and cannot offer legal or financial advice.

    (That provision is clear cut. Mediators are prohibited from giving legal advice, even if they are attorneys. This begs the question: do you have to be an attorney to conduct mediations? In many jurisdictions, at the small claims court level, one does not have to be an attorney. However, all mediators may be required to: take special courses, meet certain standards, register with their local state authority governing these issues; pay annual dues, and complete continuing education courses.
    Regarding financial advice, that too is straight forward. It is the parties themselves who must feel comfortable with a financial settlement coming out of a successful mediation, without the influence of the mediator.)

4. The mediation session can be terminated at any time by the mediator or either party.

    (Even though either party has the right to terminate, if the mediator sees an opportunity for resolution, he or she will ascertain if the party clearly wishes to go no further. The mediator may review the positive aspects that have been accomplished to that point before ending the mediation session. Too often, emotions step in front of logic and the parties end up with a court ruling that is less desirable than one that could have been accomplished had they been somewhat more flexible during the mediation.)

5. Both parties are free to consult legal counsel at any time, should they choose, especially concerning any agreement that is reduced to writing.

(If either party is pro se, and can quickly reach an attorney on the phone during the short span of the mediation, most mediators will be happy to allow the time. But, when the mediation is being conducted in the courthouse on the same day as the trial is scheduled, this is difficult to accomplish.
It is also important to note that in a number of cases, one party at mediation can be represented by an attorney and the other not. This situation has no bearing on the mediator maintaining neutrality. Attorneys are professionals at dealing with conflict and often see the benefits to a settlement coming out of mediation.)

6. Any mediated agreement, once signed, can have a significant effect upon the rights of the parties and the status of the case.

   (Parties are generally urged to only enter into an agreement that they can and will live up to. If one party breaches an agreement that was reached voluntarily during mediation and wind up back in court, that party will face an additional hurdle to winning a favorable ruling.)

7. The mediator has an obligation to report any abuse issues that may arise during the mediation process.

   (A portion of this was covered in the discussion following provision #1 regarding confidentiality. For those mediations conducted in the courthouse, in the unlikely event there are abuse issues during the conference, mediators are instructed to stop the process and call for a deputy. At that point, it could become a criminal matter for the offender.)

8. There may be times when the mediator feels that a "caucus" is needed. This is when the mediator will meet with each party separately for clarification of issues. During caucus, the parties may choose to disclose confidential information with the mediator. Such information will not be shared with the other party unless permission of the disclosing party is obtained.

(This aspect to mediation can be very productive for the parties. During caucus, not only do the parties have the opportunity to share their feelings more candidly, but just as significantly, reveal what they really want as an outcome and possibly make the initial offer for resolution. Very often it's not money. In a recent mediation that I conducted, a party was suing for $5,000 because she was "disrespected." The final resolution involved an apology letter from the defendant and an agreement by the plaintiff not to speak disparagingly about the defendant.

Sometimes it takes meeting with each party privately a number of times in order to iron out all the areas of disagreement before getting everyone in the same room once again.)

I have read and understand the above guidelines for mediation. I affirmed by participation that I have the capacity to conduct good-faith negotiations and make a decision for myself, including a decision to terminate the mediation if necessary.

(All those present at the mediation - parties, non-parties, attorneys - must sign the Guidelines in order to be in the conference room.)

GETTING STARTED

As stated, the format for mediation is fairly well established. After the guidelines are signed, the mediator will outline the ensuing process, which will include: **opening statements** by both parties, followed by **joint discussion**, **caucus**, a **reconvening** after the conclusion of caucus, and if the parties have reached a resolution, **drafting agreements**. When the parties cannot come to a mutually acceptable agreement, they are said to have reached an **impasse**. As there are nuances to each of these facets, they will be discussed individually.

As you read about this process, it is important to note that mediators have their individual style. However, they do share the ability to listen well and are intent on helping the parties resolve their dispute. Should you participate in a mediation conference, keep in mind that your mediator's approach may vary from mine.

Just prior to beginning the mediation itself, I will ask both parties to remain silent and expressionless during their opponents opening statement, even though they will hear comments they believe to be false or distasteful.

Opening Statement – The plaintiff is asked to speak first. The purpose of their overview is to state the reasons for the lawsuit, in chronological order. Time permitting, the plaintiff may be allowed to provide more background, which can sometimes reveal a key component to their true concerns. Is it is also vital to learn from the plaintiff specifically how much they are suing for and an itemization as to how the dollars are allocated. Most important is to very carefully review and pass along to the defendant all the evidence (contracts, pictures, receipts, letters, emails, etc.) in the plaintiff's possession. During the opening statement, I will be carefully listening, asking questions for clarification and taking notes. After the plaintiff is finished making their statement, I will ask the other parties for the plaintiff if they have anything to add.

The defendant is then asked to respond with their version of the facts. They may wish to counter the plaintiff's remarks directly or present their side of the story in a similar chronological manner. As long as the parties do not become argumentative, the manner in which the defendant presents his or her side is optional. For those cases where there is a countersuit, it is more productive, in my view, to address those issues after the defendant completely addresses the plaintiffs' claims. As with the plaintiff, any parties for the defendant in the room will be asked if they wish to speak. (Quite often, an attorney representing either party will opt to make the opening statement on behalf of his or her client(s). That approach is totally up to them.)

When both parties have completed their opening statements and exchanged all evidence, it's time to move to the next step.

Joint Discussion – As the name implies, this is the time during the mediation when the parties can speak directly with one another for the first time. To begin, mediators will frequently summarize what was heard from both parties during their opening statements. As a result of hearing from both sides, questions may surface that require clarification of conflicting facts.

Based on the flow of dialogue, a clear picture of all the evidence, and a perceived attitude shift, a mediator may ask, at this point, if the parties have any suggestions for resolution of the issues. A positive response could lead to immediate negotiations, with a successful conclusion in sight.

Just as often, however, the parties are still not ready to negotiate. There may be a number of unresolved issues still on the table, uncertainty about any potential offer, or a continuing hostility among the parties. Whatever the case, this would be the time to call for a caucus.

Caucus – It should be made crystal clear to both sides that the selection of who meets with the mediator first, or the time afforded the private meeting, has nothing to do with one side being favored. The mediator is absolutely neutral and will make the decision based on what is felt to be the best road to resolution.

In the privacy of a caucus, new information may surface that could affect the party's decision to settle in mediation. Also, serious conversation regarding the options for final settlement amounts and possible payment plans may take place. Where there are non-monetary issues to be resolved, ideas are often exchanged with the mediator that may satisfy both sides.

A similar scenario usually takes place when the mediator caucuses with the opponent. Once there are serious offers put on the table, it may take a series of caucuses to reach a final agreement. Once this happens, it then becomes time to reconvene with all the parties.

Unfortunately, the caucuses can bring an end to the mediation as well. In spite of this, the mediator may still reconvene the parties.

Reconvening – When the parties are brought back together, the discussion will take one of three directions: further conversation about the issues; a review to understand agreement terms; a decision that the mediation is at an impasse.

There may be a valid reason to review, once again, the issues covered during the initial joint discussions. It might even lead to another set of caucuses, which in turn, could result in a successful mediation.

When total agreement has been reached, the discussion will lead to the types of documents required to memorialize all the issues.

The reconvening of the parties could also be a very short meeting when the result has been an impasse.

Drafting the Agreement(s) - Each phase of the mediation process can be regarded as important, but how the documents are drafted is crucial. These documents will represent a culmination of all the conditions that were agreed to after carefully considered negotiations. For that reason, they must be detailed and accurate. A seasoned mediator can be invaluable in recording the proper information in a fashion that will be legally binding, especially when both parties are pro se.

Specificity is the key. If the settlement revolves around money issues only, the total amount must be indisputable. Payment plans, if applicable, must detail the amounts to be paid, due dates, sources of funds (checks, money orders, cash, etc.), method of payment (U.S. mail, wire, hand delivery, etc.), recipient's complete address. If late fees and interest are a condition of the settlement, their terms must be spelled out as well.

For those agreements that include an exchange of property, the details of the arrangement must be clearly spelled out in writing. The resulting document should include: a description of the property; the names of the parties making the exchange; and the address, time, and place where the exchange will take place.

When labor is to be performed in order to resolve the dispute, the resulting document should include: a complete and detailed description of the work; the name(s) of those to perform the work; and the start and completion date.

Your mediator, in all probability, will initially outline all the terms and conditions agreed upon. Upon agreement by the parties that everything is included, the drafting of the final agreement can begin.

A successful mediation will yield one or a combination of the following agreements: a **Consent Agreement** (figure 1 – pg. 112); a **Consent Judgment** (figure 2 – pg. 113); a **Consent Order** (figure 3 – pg. 114-115); and a **Dismissal** (figure 4 – pg. 116). Parties can also agree to a **Continuance**.

The **Consent Agreement** is the broadest of the agreements in that it can include both money to be paid and all the conditions regarding the exchange of goods or services, labor (to complete a job), and any other terms that are legal and specific.

A major benefit in small claims court to entering into a consent agreement, as opposed to a consent judgment, is that once all the conditions are met, the case will be dismissed.

There are time limits, however, as directed by the policies of the court in your jurisdiction. Generally, if all the terms can be met within a six-month period, a consent agreement will work. The reason for the time constraints is that a consent agreement will include a continuance with another date for a hearing. When all the conditions are met, the case will be dismissed. On the other hand, going through a trial after breaching a consent agreement could be a difficult challenge for the offender.

To see what form a Consent Agreement takes, I have, once again, used the wording made available to the public by the Cobb County Magistrate Court. In other jurisdictions, this wording may vary.

Unlike a Consent Agreement, payment terms are open ended in a **Consent Judgment.** But, it is an instrument designed for money awards only. It must also be noted that the party owing the money is consenting to a judgment, with all its attending liabilities. Even though the court does not distribute a list of judgments, should a credit agency check with the court, the information will become available to them. This, in all likelihood, would negatively impact someone's credit. Should the obligations under the judgment not be met by the debtor, the person owed the money will have a number of collection options. (More about this topic will be discussed in the next section of the book.)

Even when payment terms cannot be worked out due to an inability or lack of a desire to make a commitment for specific payment terms, the losing party can still consent to the judgment. In this manner, the parties can avoid a trial and may save time by having all the paperwork done during mediation.

It is important to note that judgments have to be signed by a judge. Generally, Consent Judgements cannot be appealed.

For educational purposes, I have also included a sample of a Consent Judgment form that is used for the public by the Cobb County Magistrate Court.

At times, the parties come to full agreement regarding all financial aspects of their dispute, but the defendant is reluctant to settle the case when faced with the burden of a judgment. In such instances, depending on the jurisdiction, an alternative to a Consent Judgment could be that of a **Consent Order**. While both documents are orders of the court and require a judge's signature, a major difference between them is that no judgment will be issued against the defendant unless he or she fails to meet the terms contained within the Consent Order. Should that take place, with a sworn affidavit filed with the court; a plaintiff can then obtain a judgment. Generally, Consent Orders cannot be appealed. To learn more about this document, a sample of a typically worded Consent Order is included with the other forms.

One possible result of a successful mediation is a **dismissal** (or mutual dismissal in a countersuit) of the lawsuit. The forms used for this purpose are quite simple. A key term used in a dismissal is *without prejudice* (no bar to bringing a lawsuit). If that is not the intent of the party, it can be changed to *with prejudice* (barred from bring an action on the same claim) depending on the desire of the party signing the dismissal. Figure 3 is reflective of the form used for a dismissal, again by the Cobb County Magistrate Court.

Due to the complexities of some mediated settlements, it may become necessary to use a combination of all these forms – the consent agreement, consent judgment, and the dismissal.

Your mediator will explain how the forms will be integrated, and assist in drafting each of them.

Impasse – Much of the discussion about mediation is centered on a successful outcome. But even using the success rate in Cobb County of about 70%, it also means that 30% come to an impasse. The chief cause of an impasse is the parties finding themselves too far apart to compromise. Occasionally, the party appearing doesn't have the authority to negotiate the amount of dollars under discussion. In one such case, I found myself on a cell phone during caucus with the owner of a company in an attempt to reach an agreement. And, it actually worked to the benefit of both parties. The more frustrating cases are those where one party agrees to mediate, but has absolutely no intention of settling. Upon being questioned when an impasse became the only option, the answer was that they didn't care to offend the judge by saying no to mediation. Another frequent response is that they didn't understand what mediation was. Nevertheless, while some mediation conferences may not successfully reach a written agreement, in most cases the time spent is productive in terms of preparation for the trial. This completes the discussion on court-related mediation with "impasse" being the final outcome before going to trial.

***

As the previous discussion centered on mediation conferences as part of the process after a calendar call, it is important to note that a **private mediation** can always be conducted either before filing a lawsuit or prior to an appearance in court once a lawsuit has been filed.

The first challenge in attempting to resolve a dispute through private mediation is for the parties to initially agree on the concept. Other than those benefits directly associated court-related mediation, most apply to private mediation too.

Assuming the parties agree to mediation, the next step is to engage a mediator acceptable to both sides. There are a number of sources to assist in this endeavor such as: the Association for Conflict Resolution; the Alternative Dispute Resolution supervisor at your local courthouse; or the governing authority over mediators in your State. For disputes that involve more complex legal issues and/or instances where the damages sought are significant, you might consider contacting a mediation law firm.

Regarding the costs for a private mediation, unless contractually specified otherwise, most often all expenses are shared equally by the parties. Mediators bill by the hour and sometimes require a minimum number of hours. The hourly rate for cases typically headed for small claims court will range from $250 to $450 per hour. Other costs may include reimbursement for facility fees (e.g. conference rooms) and administrative fees for generating and distributing settlement documents.

The goal for both parties in a private mediation should be a complete and final resolution of all issues in their dispute. If achieved prior to filing a suit, a detailed Consent Agreement can be written, dated, and signed. While this document is not an order of the court, it can become an important piece of evidence in a subsequent lawsuit should the terms and conditions not be fully met by either or both sides.

When an agreement has been reached after a lawsuit has been filed, all financial matters can be detailed in either a Consent Judgment or Consent Order. Non-monetary issues can be included in a Consent Agreement. Should the parties need more time to finalize the document(s), and both parties are agreeable, a continuance can be requested of the judge. Most often it will be granted, especially if this is the first request.

CONDUCT DURING TRIAL

Once the trial begins, strict rules must be adhered to. The following suggestions are based on instructions that I either heard directly from judges during their pre-calendar call remarks or from my observations while sitting in the courtroom. For clarity, the information is broken down into three behavioral categories – **overall behavior**, **behavior before the judge**, and **behavior during testimony**.

Overall behavior – Controlling your body language is crucial. Judges will not permit rolling of the eyes, smirking, shaking of the head, grunts, moans, or other gestures. Other than when you are called to testify, remain silent and still. This goes for your witnesses, as well.

Tugging at your attorney's sleeve is not only disturbing to the court, but a distraction to a professional who is trained to listen to every word during the preceding.

Behavior before the judge – Violating any of the following may place you in a position with the judge in which no party wishes to find himself. Always address the judge as "Your Honor," no exceptions. Just as significantly, never speak when the judge is speaking. Always answer a judge's question directly and never lie. Doing so may damage your case beyond repair and you could be cited for *perjury* (knowingly making a false statement during a judicial proceeding), which is a criminal offense. If you are seated at the counsel's table, as opposed to standing in the well or seated in the witness box, it is recommended that you stand when addressing the judge.

Behavior during testimony – Your testimony can be as vital to winning your case as the evidence submitted to the court. To place yourself in a favorable position, the following suggestions can be very helpful.

- Speak in a sincere manner and never be argumentative or sarcastic.
- Never ramble, stick to the facts and be brief. Avoid repetition; judges are trained listeners and take notes during the proceeding.
- When stating facts, like dates, times, dollar amounts, be exact. It's okay if you are not sure, but say so. In the same light, when answering questions from the judge, your attorney, or your opponent, if you are not sure of the answer or can't remember, say so.
- Unless you are cross-examining, never speak directly to your opponent.
- When cross-examining your opponent or their witnesses, only ask questions. Do not make statements.
- Do not use obscene language or profanity. The only exception to this recommendation might be when you must use a direct quote of foul language that is

absolutely germane to the suit. Still, I would apologize to the court prior to making the statement.

- Be absolutely still and show no emotion when your opponent or their witnesses are testifying. Not observing this rule will annoy the judge and can be damaging to your case.
- Never argue with a judge after a ruling has been handed down.

Objection - When an *objection* (a motion made to disallow evidence or testimony by a witness) is made, everyone must stop talking so that the judge can decide the legal relevance and either sustain or overrule the objection. **An objection must have a basis in law** and not simply an expression of negativity toward your opponent's evidence or testimony.

TRIAL PROCEDURE

Civil Court - It might be very worthwhile for you, as a party to a lawsuit, to visit a small claims court, when in session, in advance of your trial. In this manner, you will be able to become more familiar and comfortable with the process. For those who cannot or choose not to do this, the following portrays the sequence of events that you can expect once the case is called for a hearing by the judge.

As the discussion of trial procedure begins, it must be noted that the process itself changes somewhat when one or both parties are represented by an attorney. His or her role is to take the lead by making the opening and closing statements. The attorneys will control the flow of testimony by asking questions of their client, while simultaneously presenting evidence. Witnesses will be treated in exactly the same manner. When applicable, they may object to an opponent's testimony and/or evidence cross-examine the other side.

Even though they may present a very strong argument on behalf of their clients, good attorneys will not only be respectful to the judge, but extend that courtesy to the opposing parties and their attorneys.

To depict the actual trial process for learning purposes, the assumption is that you will be going to court pro se. Previously covered was the manner in which you should conduct yourself and present well organized labeled evidence. The key during your presentation, once again, is to be brief, stick to the facts, present all your significant evidence, and stay within the time constraints of your announcement. (Keep in mind, the time you requested to present your case, including the potential of cross examination and a closing statement.)

After you have indicated to the judge that your testimony is complete, your opponent will be asked if they have any questions of you. Your answers should be brief, accurate, and on point; no more, no less. Even if you detest the other party, it is in your best interest to act in a proper manner all through the trial.

If you have witnesses to support your position, their testimony will follow yours. They too will be subject to cross examination.

Immediately following the testimony of the plaintiff's side, the defendant (and witnesses, if applicable) will counter with his or her own testimony and evidence. As you were questioned by your opponent, you will have the same opportunity to cross examine. Be aware, you will be limited to questions only; no statements or opinions will be permitted. If you violate this, particularly more than once, you may be reprimanded by the judge. To remain credible, you should stay within the rules and conduct yourself professionally.

After both sides have presented their arguments, including cross examination, time permitting, the judge may ask each party if they have anything else to add in rebuttal. If nothing surfaces to counter the opponent's testimony, it's okay to simply tell the judge you have nothing more.

The last step before a ruling is handed down is the presentation of closing arguments. While there is no requirement to make one, it might be beneficial to review your case with salient points and let the judge know specifically why the ruling should be in your favor.

For the majority of cases, the judge will hand down the ruling from the bench. This means you will get a decision in a matter of minutes. Some judges will go to the extent of explaining in some detail the reasoning behind the decision. Others will be brief in their explanation or simply announce the amount of the money award to the winner. There is always a chance that a judge will dismiss a plaintiff's case, and do the same for a counterclaim. That is why a trial can be a lose-lose for both parties.

Some cases yield a large amount of evidence to be reviewed by the judge or involve complex issues of law. In those instances, the judge may take your case *under advisement* (allow time to render a decision). In small claims court, it generally means that you will learn the judge's decision by mail within a two-week period.

JUDGE'S RULING

At the conclusion of a hearing, the judge's ruling can be: a **Judgment for the Plaintiff** (figure 5 – pg. 117), a **Default Judgment** (figure 6 – pg. 118), a **Judgment for the Defendant** (figure 7 – pg. 119), a **Judgment on the Counterclaim** (figure 8 – pg. 120) or a **"Wash" Order** (figure 9 – pg. 121). Other than the parties to a suit, their attorneys, and court personnel, most people are not familiar with the format of a judge's order. The wording depicted on the subsequent forms reflects those that are rendered in the Magistrate Court of Cobb County. Other jurisdictions may use language that differs somewhat from these.

POST-TRIAL

Obnoxious post-trial conduct, in or outside the courtroom, could cause problems for the offending party. As difficult as it might be to lose, remain dignified as you exit the courtroom and lobby. I witnessed a situation where the mother of the plaintiff, who had just lost a case, began cursing and screaming at the prevailing party. Hearing the disturbance, the deputy emerged from the courtroom and came close to arresting the woman.

If you are concerned about your safety, talk to the deputy. It can be arranged for one party to remain in the courthouse while the other leaves or you may be provided with an escort to your car.

****

DISPOSSESSION COURT
(a.k.a. EVICTION COURT)

While there are similarities between small claims court and dispossession court, there are also differences. First among them is that no dollar limit is placed on a landlord's claim in this court. Also, the cases heard in dispossession court are limited to disputes over occupancy, rent, late fees, claims for utilities, and early lease termination, etc. (Typically the two types of real estate issues heard in small claims court are those dealing with claims over damage to property and non-payment of rent under a Lease- Purchase Agreement.)

The objective of landlords in this court is to get a writ of possession for their property and a judgment for money owed to them through the last day of occupancy by the tenant. However, quite often both the landlord and tenant will work out an agreed to repayment plan as part of an arrangement that allows the tenant to remain in the property.

In order for a case to be heard by a judge in dispossession court, there is a condition regarding the acceptance of money that must be met by the landlord. If money was accepted during the month the case was filed, there is a strong possibility that the case will be dismissed and will need to be refiled. Landlords, who are aware of this provision, will come to court with non-cashed checks or money orders. Two sticky areas regarding collection of rent that are problematic for landlords are rent payments made via direct deposit and accepting the government's portion of Section 8 leases, even when the tenants portion has not been paid. In those cases, arrangements should be made so that no money is received during the filing month.

On court day, as with small claims court, both the landlord and tenant must appear. Keep in mind that only the listed parties on the lease (or their attorney) can represent themselves at trial. Co-owners, parties with a power of attorney, and spouses will not be permitted to appear for a named party.

Should neither the landlord nor tenant answer the calendar call, the case will be dismissed. Likewise, if the tenant appears and the landlord does not, the case will also be dismissed. On the other hand, if the tenant doesn't show up, but admitted the claim, the judge will generally grant to the landlord an immediate writ and a judgment for the full claim. Using the same scenario, but where the tenant denied the claim, the landlord will be asked to appear before the judge, present the evidence and give testimony to prove the claim. If the judge agrees, the judgment and a writ will be granted.

As with most disputes, both the landlord and tenant have an obligation under the law to make a good faith effort to resolve their differences before a trial. If mediators are available, the parties can avail themselves of assistance through a mediation conference.

The manner in which a mediation conference in dispossession court is conducted mirrors that of small claims court, with some subtle differences. After going through the preliminaries, including the guidelines, the very first question a mediator may ask is whether there is any reason to discuss the tenant remaining in the property, under terms to be agreed upon by both parties. This decision rests first with the landlord, and if acceptable, with the tenant, who may or may not want to stay. One needs to clarify this issue at the outset of mediation because it not only adds another dimension to a subsequent written agreement, but dramatically changes the attitudes of the parties. Under these circumstances, a Consent Judgment may be coupled with a Consent Agreement to cover other issues that may be a part of the new arrangement.

In either case, tenants remaining or leaving, the very next issue to be discussed is whether both the landlord and tenant agree that a valid lease exists. (If they don't, it makes the mediation and any appearance before a judge more challenging for the parties). I will always hand the lease to the tenant to establish its authenticity. By doing this, my goal is to get beyond any disputes having to do with the terms of the lease. When the lease has expired and the tenant is residing in the property on a month-to-month basis, it is important to establish whether or not there was a continuation clause. An acknowledgment by the tenant, in this regard, eliminates debate as to whether or not the lease still governed the tenancy.

(A number of cases heard in dispossession court are "tenancy at will" cases, where both the landlord and tenant agree for the tenant to occupy the property on a month to month basis. This arrangement can come about as a result of the expiration of a lease or by an oral agreement at the beginning of occupancy with a new tenant. Regardless of how it came about, the eviction process is the same for the landlord as if there were a lease in force.)

Once the validity of the lease question is settled, the next objective is to establish an agreed-to amount of money owed by the tenant. When filing, some dispossession courts require the landlord to complete a form that clearly depicts the claim. Often, it will be broken down by month and year, separating the rent from late fees and other money due the landlord under the terms of the lease. In this manner, the tenant (and the judge) has the opportunity to see exactly how the total claim has been allocated. Sometimes the tenant, after reviewing this form, acknowledges an amount owed and the discussion then becomes one of structuring an agreeable and affordable payment plan.

When there is disagreement about the amount of money owed, the tenant can point to specific areas of concern. The negotiation can then focus on each of the specific items and corresponding dollar amounts brought up by the tenant. Either there will be an agreement, or the mediation will be at an impasse, and the case will be headed for the courtroom.

From the positive side, when there is an agreement on the total dollars owed, the discussion may turn toward structuring a workable payment plan to discharge the debt. The major hurdle here for the landlord and tenant is to agree on terms that fulfill one party's goal for accelerated repayment and the other's need for payments low enough to cover their future rent and overhead. It takes compromise by both sides to achieve this.

Some tenants will either refuse mediation altogether or won't agree to any compromise offered them by the landlord, because they insist upon seeing the judge. This is especially true when they believe they have an arguable position as to why the rent has not been paid. If their position is credible, like provable conditions that made the property uninhabitable, the judge may take that into consideration. Tenants sometimes believe that their personal financial hardships will sway the judge. While sympathetic, the decision by the judge will be guided by the law.

An area where the judge does have discretion is over excessive late charges. Even if covered in the lease, the judge may reduce or eliminate late fees that are deemed unreasonable.

Another reason a tenant may wish to go before the judge is to plead for remaining in the property for more than seven days. The law in Georgia allows for a maximum of seven days and that is all the judge will grant. Thus, the landlord will receive a writ of possession on the eighth day.

The losing party in Dispossession Court, as with all other courts, has the right of appeal. Those requirements will be discussed in the next section of the book.

Figure 1: Consent Agreement

(Sample Only)

IN THE MAGISTRATE COURT OF _____ COUNTY
STATE OF _____

CONSENT AGREEMENT

Plaintiff

vs.   Civil Action Number _____

Defendant

In the mediation session conducted on this date, the parties in the above styled action hereby mutually agree and consent to the following:

The Defendant, _____ , agrees to pay the Plaintiff, _____ , $ ____ in full and final settlement of the above action. Said amount will be paid via _____ .

(Non-monetary terms specified here)

The Plaintiff has been provided a Dismissal form and agrees to dismiss this case once the above conditions are satisfied. This case is rescheduled for a contested hearing on **(date & time). All parties understand that they must attend this hearing unless the Plaintiff's claim has been dismissed. Failure to appear will result in an automatic dismissal of the case.** Once dismissed, the case will be removed from the calendar and a copy of the *Dismissal* will be sent to both parties.

The parties confirm, by signing below, that they are signing this document voluntarily and of their own free will. Further, they acknowledge that they received no legal advice from the mediator during the mediation session and they are not signing this agreement under duress or coercion of any sort. It is also agreed that the parties were afforded the opportunity to have this matter formally heard today in court and that they are willing to postpone the hearing in order for the conditions of this agreement to be satisfied.

This _____ day of _____, 20___.

_____   _____
Plaintiff   Attorney for Plaintiff*

_____   _____
Defendant   Attorney for Defendant*

* If parties are represented by an attorney

Figure 2: Consent Judgment

(Sample Only)

IN THE MAGISTRATE COURT OF _____ COUNTY
STATE OF _____

CONSENT JUDGMENT

Plaintiff

vs.   Civil Action Number _____

Defendant

The Plaintiff and the Defendant agree that a judgment shall be entered in this case, as evidenced by the signatures below. It is hereby ordered and adjudged that said judgment be rendered in favor of the Plaintiff and against the Defendant for the sum of $ _____ PRINCIPAL and $ _____ COURT COSTS.

Parties further agree that the Defendant shall be allowed to make payments on this indebtedness at the rate of $ _____ (weekly) (bi-weekly) (monthly) with the first payment being due and payable on _____ , and each subsequent payment shall be due (weekly) (bi-weekly) (monthly) thereafter until the balance is paid in full. There shall be no penalty for prepayments. The plaintiff agrees to notify the Clerk of the Magistrate Court in writing once the Defendant has satisfied the judgment.

No Fi Fa will issue and no garnishment or other action will be taken on said judgment as long as payments are timely begun and timely paid, as agreed. Should the defendant fail to make a payment or should payment be made more than three (3) days beyond the due date, the clerk of magistrate court shall issue a Fi Fa in the amount then outstanding. Plaintiff will give written notice to the clerk that payments have not been made as agreed and the amount unpaid.

All payments should be made to (Plaintiffs name and address)

_____

This _____ day of _____ , 20____ .

                                        _____
                                        Judge, Magistrate Court

CONSENTED TO:

_____
Plaintiff

_____
Defendant

Figure 3: Consent Order

(Sample Only)

IN THE MAGISTRATE COURT OF _____ COUNTY
STATE OF _____

Plaintiff

vs.   Civil Action Number _____

Defendant

CONSENT ORDER

Plaintiff and Defendant in the above action show this Court their consent and agreement as follows:

1.

Defendant agrees to pay plaintiff the total sum of $_____ as settlement in full off this lawsuit.

2.

Parties further agree Defendant shall be allowed to make payments on this indebtedness at the rate of $_____ (weekly) (biweekly) (monthly), with the first payment being due and payable on _____ and subsequent payments being due (weekly) (biweekly) (monthly) thereafter.

3.

When Defendant has paid all amounts required under the terms of this Consent Order, Plaintiff shall dismiss this lawsuit with prejudice.

4.

Should Defendant default pursuant to the terms of this agreement, Plaintiff shall notify Defendant of such default, in writing via certified mail with return receipt requested, allowing Defendant a five (5) day "grace period" in which to cure said the default. Said five (5) day "grace period" will commence as of the date the certified receipt is returned to the Plaintiff.

5.

Should the Defendant fail to cure said default within the five (5) day "grace period", plaintiff shall be entitled, without further notice to Defendant and upon submission of an affidavit of default by Plaintiff to the Court, to have ex-parte judgment entered against the Defendant for the principal sum of $_____ less any payments made pursuant to this agreement, plus post-judgment interest pursuant to _____, plus all costs of this action. Defendant expressly waives notice of the entry of a default judgment as may be required by law or court rules.

(Page 1 of 2)

Figure 3: Consent Order – *Continued*

6.

In the event the Court fails to receive a request from the Plaintiff for a dismissal or ex-parte judgment, the case will automatically be dismissed after 30 days of the final payment's due date.

THEREFORE, it appearing to this Court that the parties hereto are in agreement with the terms and conditions as set forth here in;

IT IS HEREBY ORDERED that this agreement become an Order of the Court and the parties are directed to strictly comply herewith.

This _____ day of _____, _____ .

_____
Judge, Magistrate Court

CONSENTED TO:

_____
Plaintiff

_____
Defendant

Figure 4: Dismissal of Claim/Counterclaim

(Sample Only)

IN THE MAGISTRATE COURT OF _____ COUNTY
STATE OF _____

Dismissal of Claim

Plaintiff

vs.   Civil Action Number _____

Defendant

The plaintiff(s) in the above styled action does hereby voluntarily dismiss his claim without prejudice against _____ .

.

This the _____ day of _____ , 20___ .

_____
Plaintiff

Dismissal of Counterclaim*

The defendant in the above styled action does hereby voluntarily dismiss his counterclaim without prejudice against _____ .

This the _____ day of _____ , 20___ .

_____
Defendant

* Used only when there is a counterclaim

Figure 5: Judgment for the Plaintiff

(Sample Only)

IN THE MAGISTRATE COURT OF _____ COUNTY
STATE OF _____

Plaintiff

vs.   Civil Action Number _____

Defendant

JUDGMENT

The within case having been tried, and after hearing evidence I find in favor of the Plaintiff, _____, on the main claim.

It is hereby **ORDERED** and **DECREED** that the plaintiff, _____, do have and recover from the defendant, _____, the sum of $ ____ dollars as principal, $ _____ dollars as interest to date, $ _____ dollars as attorney's fees*; together with future interest* at the rate equal to prime rate as published on the date of this Judgment plus 3 percent and $ ____ dollars court cost.

So **ORDERED**, this the ____ day of _____, 20___.

_____
Judge, Magistrate Court

* Attorney's fees and/or interest may not apply in all cases

Figure 6: Judgment by Default

(Sample Only)

IN THE MAGISTRATE COURT OF _____ COUNTY
STATE OF _____

Plaintiff

vs.   Civil Action Number _____

Defendant

JUDGMENT BY DEFAULT

It appearing to the Court that proper notice of trial having been given to all parties, and the defendant having failed to answer the call of the calendar in open court, therefore, the answer of the defendant is dismissed.

The Court further finds that, after hearing evidence from the plaintiff, that a Judgment by Default be awarded to the plaintiff.

It is **ORDERED**, that the Plaintiff, _____, do have and recover from the Defendant, _____, the sum of $_____ dollars principal, $_____ dollars interest*, and $_____ dollars attorney's fees*; together with future interest* at the rate equal to prime as published on the date of this Judgment plus 3 and $ _____ dollars court costs.

So **ORDERED**, this the ____ day of _____, 20___.

_____
Judge, Magistrate Court

* Attorney's fees and/or interest may not apply in all cases

Figure 7: Judgment for Defendant

(Sample Only)

IN THE MAGISTRATE COURT OF _____ COUNTY
STATE OF _____

Plaintiff

vs.   Civil Action Number _____

Defendant

JUDGMENT FOR DEFENDANT

After hearing evidence from both parties, it is hereby **ORDERED** that the judgment rendered in favor of the Defendant(s), against the Plaintiff(s), and that the cost be assessed against the plaintiff.

So **ORDERED**, this the _____ day of _____, 20___.

_____
Judge, Magistrate Court

Figure 8: Judgment on the Counterclaim

(Sample Only)

IN THE MAGISTRATE COURT OF _____ COUNTY
STATE OF _____

Plaintiff

vs.   Civil Action Number _____

Defendant

JUDGMENT

   The within case having been tried, and after hearing evidence I find in favor of the Defendant, _____ on the counterclaim.

   It is hereby ORDERED and DECREED that the Defendant _____ do have and recover from the Plaintiff _____, the sum of $ _____ dollars as principal, $ _____ dollars as interest* to date, $ _____ dollars as attorney's fees*; together with future interest* at the rate equal to prime rate as published on the date of this Judgment plus 3 percent and $ _____ dollars court cost.

        So **ORDERED**, this the ____ day of _____, 20___.

_____
Judge, Magistrate Court

* Attorney's fees and/or interest may not apply in all cases

Figure 9: "Wash" Order

(Sample Only)

IN THE MAGISTRATE COURT OF _____ COUNTY
STATE OF _____

Plaintiff

vs.   Civil Action Number _____

Defendant

ORDER

The within case having been tried between the parties and after hearing evidence, I find in favor of the defendant _____ on the main claim;

IT IS FURTHER ORDERED that I find in favor of the plaintiff, _____, on the counterclaim, with all costs being assessed against the plaintiff.

So **ORDERED**, this the _____ day of _____, 20___.

_____
Judge, Magistrate Court

121

The prevailing party in a lawsuit now faces the challenge of collecting their judgment. At the same time, the losing party may be considering an appeal. These issues will be addressed in the next section, titled "Pursuing."

Pursuing

After a ruling is handed down by a judge, the options for the parties are clearly defined, depending on which side you find yourself. The winner's sole objective is to collect on the judgment. The losing side must pay it, take other action, or face the consequences of ignoring an order of the court.

WINNING SIDE

Collecting your judgment very often is more tedious and frustrating than what you may have experienced during the entire process from preparation to trial. To reach a positive conclusion and collect the money that is due you, it might be helpful to prepare a written plan of action. In structuring a plan, your goal should be to collect on the debt as quickly and painlessly as possible. Your options are: securing a **payment plan**, **garnishment**, and/or acting on a *Fi.Fa.* (Fieri Facia - Latin term referring to authorizing a sheriff, with a writ of execution, to seize goods or property). Your approach may be influenced or directed by whether your opponent is an individual or business. Regardless, a determination of the other party's financial wherewithal will direct the tactic you may take to secure payment.

If some level of communication still exists with your opponent after the trial, an arrangement should be made immediately to meet and discuss payment. It may be somewhat easier if your opponent is a viable business rather than an individual. The owners may be motivated to quickly discharge the obligation and have the judgment satisfied so as not to negatively impact their company. In dealing with an individual, payment may be more difficult to obtain, but it is certainly worth the effort.

When you meet, both parties should clearly understand that you are holding all the cards. That doesn't suggest in any way that your attitude should reflect your potency. Haughtiness could be counterproductive. If the meeting goes well, you may be on your way toward a positive conclusion, and perhaps leave with some money that day. Should the party refuse to meet with you, or the meeting concludes without a satisfactory end, at least you will have the satisfaction of knowing that you did everything possible, through personal communication, to resolve the matter.

To take the next step in the collection process, it is always better to have a clear picture of the other party's ability to pay. As a holder of a judgment, you are entitled to receive from your opponent accurate and truthful information about his or her employment and finances. The legal method for obtaining the information you seek is with a **Post-Judgment** *Interrogatory* (a set of questions to be answered in writing under oath).

Post-Judgment Interrogatory (figure 10 – pg. 134) – The judgment debtor is obligated to provide you with data pertaining to: their employment and income, bank accounts (including the names and numbers of each and every account in his or her name), stocks/bonds/securities (and the value of each one), real estate holdings (including addresses, value, mortgage information), automobiles (including VIN and tag numbers, loans against the vehicles), and other possible assets (like jewelry, boats, etc.) Your local jurisdiction will provide the form necessary to obtain this information. (Figure 10, as well as the succeeding forms, are samples modeled after those furnished to the general public by the Cobb County Magistrate Court. They may differ somewhat in language from those used in your local jurisdiction, but they serve the same purpose. In any case, these forms are displayed to give you a general idea as to their format.) Once completed, the form should be sent to your opponent by certified mail or by perfection of service by the sheriff.

The debtor has a specific time within which he or she must respond to the interrogatory. Very often, it is thirty days. As you will note, there is space provided on the interrogatory for verification by the debtor that their answers are true and complete. If, upon receipt, you believe your opponent's answers to be untruthful or incomplete, there is a process by which you can go before the judge to point out the discrepancies. The judge can then order the debtor to furnish the missing or inaccurate information.

Should the debtor fail to respond to the interrogatory, a second step will be required to continue in this pursuit. It will be necessary to then file a ***Motion to Compel Discovery*** (requesting a court to order a party to answer discovery) (figure 11 – pg.

135). That document, plus a ***Rule Nisi*** (an order that a defendant appear before a judge to answer an interrogatory) (figure 12 – pg. 136) will be served upon your opponent by the sheriff.

In the event that your opponent still doesn't appear, you can then file an **Application for Citation of Contempt** (figure 13 – pg. 137). This, too, will be served by the sheriff. Failing to appear after this third step can result in the judge then signing a bench warrant for the defendant's arrest.

****

Whether you are able to secure the information you need to collect on the debt voluntarily or by the above described method, the next step(s) available to you as the judgment holder are **garnishment** and/or liens and seizure of property with a **Fi.Fa.**

***Garnishment* (an order granted to withhold money or attach property to repay a debt obligation)** - Utilized by judgment holders as a primary method to collect a debt, there are some basics that should be understood by anyone contemplating garnishment.

While it may seem obvious, you must have a judgment in order to file a garnishment. (The exceptions are the Internal Revenue Service or State tax authorities, who can garnish for unpaid taxes. Other Federal agencies can also garnish wages for any debt owed to the United States.)

The two most common forms of garnishment are a Regular Garnishment, used primarily for garnishing a bank account, and a Continuing Garnishment, used only for garnishing wages. As for the latter, most states, including Georgia, permit this type of garnishment. However, there are four states (South Carolina, North Carolina, Pennsylvania, and Texas) that prohibit any form of wage garnishment except for debts associated with taxes, federally guaranteed student loans, child support and court-ordered restitution or fines.

In order to exercise a garnishment, fees must be paid, and they may vary from county to county, state to state. These fees can run into the hundreds of dollars, depending upon where the garnishment is being filed and which services you are requesting. For example, if you ask for both the defendant and *garnishee* (holder of the funds), to be served by the Sheriff's Department, it will be more costly than handling a portion of the service by yourself. Any mailed summons must be sent via Registered mail with Return Receipt Requested.

In addition to paying the required fees, there are a number of forms that must be completed, signed and notarized (or signed in front of a court clerk). These forms may have different names, depending on the jurisdiction, but in general they are: an **Affidavit** (which may be a multiple copy form); a **Garnishee's Summons and Answer Form**; a **Defendant's Copy of Summons**; and a **Sheriff's Entry of Service**. If an attorney is not assisting you, it might be worthwhile to get help completing the forms at the courthouse. The clerks will not give you legal advice, but can review each form to be sure they are properly completed. (Samples of these forms are not being displayed due to their comprehensiveness and format.)

Once served, the garnishee (employer, bank, etc.) has a period of time to respond, sometimes 45 days. Should they fail to answer, they could be held responsible for the entire debt.

As part of this overview, here are some facts about garnishment that may be helpful to understanding the process:

- An employee cannot be fired because of a garnishment.
- No more than 25% of the debtor's take-home pay (balance of funds after exemptions required by law) can be deducted.
- The wage garnishment can be placed for a maximum of 180 days. Should the full amount of the debt not be paid within this timeframe, another garnishment can be filed for the remaining balance.
- The wages of anyone earning less than the minimum wage cannot be garnished.
- While the court cannot guarantee payment, the money will be paid directly to the court and subsequently mailed to the judgment holder in a timely fashion.

The debtor does have the opportunity to challenge the garnishment. The process begins with the filing of what is called a **Garnishment Traverse**. The filing however, does not stop the garnishment process. These forms are available from the clerk at your local courthouse or on-line in some jurisdictions.

A court date may be scheduled as soon as two weeks after the filing. At the hearing, the judge will review the documents presented by the debtor. If deemed valid, the judge can overturn the garnishment. All funds in possession of the court at that time will then be returned to the debtor.

Fi.Fa. – In lieu of or in addition to garnishing bank accounts and/or wages, another avenue to collect on a judgment is by placing a lien and seizing personal property. This is done by first obtaining a writ of Fi.Fa. from the clerk's office in the county where the judgment was awarded. If yours was granted as a default judgment, you may get the writ immediately. However, if your judgment came about after a contested hearing, there is a 10 day waiting period in Georgia.

With a Fi.Fa. in hand, the next step is to record the lien on the county's General Execution Docket. For any property located in other counties, you must have the lien recorded in each county individually. You may record liens out-of-state, but an attorney must be retained to handle this for you.

In order to have the sheriff's office place a lien on personal property, you must first have your Fi.Fa. This too will have to be done in each county where the personal property is located. To levy real property is much more complicated and may require the services of an attorney to assist you.

Filing a lien on an automobile requires an additional step. A special form for this purpose must be completed and submitted to the Georgia Department of Revenue, Motor Vehicles Division. Other states have a similar process, but it will be necessary to check with those states for the exact steps to take.

As with wage garnishment, when the debt is paid in full, the judgment holder must notify each county where the liens have been recorded.

****

If the previously described methods of collection appear to be too confusing, tedious, time-consuming or frustrating, you might consider hiring either a collection agency or a collection attorney.

Collection Agencies are professionals at tracking and collecting money owed by debtors. These firms work on either a flat fee or a percentage of money collected. At first glance, the flat fee may seem to be more attractive because your costs will be lower. However, what you may be paying for is simply a series of letters from them to your debtor. Sometimes a letter from companies such as this has positive results, but quite often the debtor will continue to resist taking care of the obligation. Albeit at a higher cost, you may be assured that the Collection Agencies working on a percentage will be more motivated and more aggressive.

Retaining an attorney that specializes in collections is a viable alternative. As you are already the judgment holder, their legal services will be focused solely on attempts to recover your debt. Their fees may be a hybrid of a small retainer to cover direct costs coupled with a percentage of the money collected. Unlike working with a collection agency, this alternative has the benefit of establishing a personal relationship with the attorney and can offer the possibility of a negotiated fee for services.

Whether you pursue collection though an agency or attorney, it is going to cost a portion of the money owed to you. If you had considered the potential of collection costs earlier in the process, might it have been better to comprise during settlement discussions prior to a trial?

LOSING SIDE

Finding yourself on the losing side of a lawsuit doesn't offer as many options as that of your opponent. While there may be others, the three most common actions you can take are: **paying the debt**, filing an **appeal**, or filing **bankruptcy**.

Paying the debt – Debts can be paid in a number of ways, as long as the method is acceptable to the judgment holder. Their preference will undoubtedly be a lump sum monetary payment for the entire debt, paid immediately. If you can afford it, getting a judgment satisfied quickly is in your best interest. For many, this option may not be possible, due to financial constraints. So, rather than go through the thorny collection process previously discussed, the judgment holder may accept a payment plan. A carefully worded Consent Agreement can protect the debt holder and obligate you, so that both parties can be working toward a resolution.

Assuming a plan that is based on cash payments is not possible; you might offer a voluntary transfer of assets as payment. The difficulty under a plan like this is that a mutual agreement must be reached regarding the value of the assets being offered. Once agreed to, a document should be generated, signed and dated, that specifically identifies and itemizes the assets being exchanged to satisfy the monetary debt.

Let us say that neither cash payments nor valuable assets are available for payment, it might be possible to offer labor in exchange for the debt. Here again, agreement as to the value of the labor should be established and acceptable to the debt holder. This type of arrangement is even more difficult to construct because it involves hourly rates, number of hours, start and completion date, etc. However, if both parties agree to this arrangement, the documentation should not be an obstacle standing in the way of a solution. It can be properly documented, but professional assistance may be required.

Whatever the method of repayment of the debt, the judgment holder has the obligation to inform the court once the judgment has been satisfied.

Appeal -The initial reaction from an unhappy party in a small claims case very often is to appeal. (For the most part, an appeal will come from the losing side. At times the prevailing party may wish to appeal the judgment if it's felt that the award was too low.) It is important to note here that only parties to a contested case can appeal, the defendant in a default judgment case cannot.

People file appeals for many reasons. One reason might be the inability to get a continuance because of incomplete evidence in hand, or a key witness not being available at the time of the trial. Another might be the feeling that a stronger argument can be made after hearing testimony and seeing the opponent's evidence. Still another is a simple disagreement with the judge's findings, however, anger and frustration with the court is a poor reason to file an appeal.

Before filing an appeal, consider the fact that a learned judge, hearing all the testimony and reviewing all the evidence, still chose not to rule in your favor. Even though small claims court is not a court of record and you'll be starting with a clean slate, you should ask yourself whether you will have a substantially better argument to present in the higher court. Because either party can request a jury trial, you will also have to assess the benefits and liabilities of that potential occurrence.

When a business chooses to file an appeal, there is a requirement to be represented by an attorney. An individual may still have the pro se option. However, the entire process is fraught with technicalities that are routine for lawyers, but can be problematic for the general public. Unless you are a highly qualified individual at filing an appeal, representing yourself in a higher court can be an extraordinary challenge. Therefore, hiring an attorney to handle your appeal is always the wiser choice.

Cost considerations should also be a major factor when considering an appeal. Attorneys will very often ask for a retainer of thousands of dollars to represent you. There are also the potential costs of depositions, drafting motions, etc., that will substantially increase your legal costs.

At best, you can measure in months the time before your case may be heard. Preparation takes longer, calendars are crowded, and other delays frequently surface when waiting for your case to be heard.

If you still feel you have a strong case, can afford it, can wait it out, and are willing to take the gamble, an appeal might be the right step for you. Your appeal will be heard in a higher court.

There is a requirement that an appeal must be filed within a specific time frame after the awarding of a judgment. As it varies from state to state, check with the clerk soon after receiving the judge's decision.

The fees associated with filing an appeal should be equal to that of the plaintiff's costs when filing the original case. There are also a number of specific forms that are available from the clerk of the court that must be completed in order to begin the process.

Before making a final decision, it might be advisable to visit State Court and sit in on a few trials to get a better idea of what you will be facing in that court. It may also cause you to rethink whether the effort to appeal will be worth it. This comment is not to discourage you from filing, but a reminder that an appeal may be far more time-consuming, costly, confusing, and emotionally taxing than the original case.

Until a hearing on the appeal is held and ruled upon, all collection efforts are put on hold.

Bankruptcy – Often used as a last resort, bankruptcy is generally filed when one's liabilities outweigh his or her assets and he or she find it impossible to meet their financial obligations. Before filing, consideration should be given to the long term negative effect it will have on one's ability to get credit. For some, there may be an ethical concern, as well. In addition, filing for bankruptcy can be costly in terms of court costs and legal fees. Nevertheless, the laws are in place to protect the debtor and are available to anyone in this situation to take advantage of when all else fails.

Bankruptcy proceedings are handled by a federal court. There are several types of bankruptcies, some designated for businesses and others for individuals. Even within that distinction, there are categories within the bankruptcy law (Chapters 7,8,11,13, for example) intended to best fit the needs of the parties filing. There are many issues concerning the advisability, feasibility, and legal requirements for filing bankruptcy. An attorney who specializes in bankruptcy law can advise you appropriately.

****

Finally, all judgment holders are required to notify the court when the debt has been satisfied. This can be accomplished by completing a **Satisfaction of Judgment** form as illustrated (figure 14 – pg. 138) which may be provided by the court. Or, in many jurisdictions, a letter to the court will be sufficient.

Figure 10: Interrogatory

(Sample Only)

IN THE MAGISTRATE COURT OF _____ COUNTY
STATE OF _____

Plaintiff	Current Civil Action File No. _____
vs.	Original Civil Action File No. _____
Defendant	County Where Original Judgment was Entered _____

INTERROGATORIES

To: _____, defendant in the above styled action:

The Plaintiff in the above styled action requests that you answer the following interrogatories separately, fully, and under oath and serve such answers on said plaintiff's address shown above by mail or hand deliver within 30 days after the service of these interrogatories.

1. List your full name, home phone number, and address, including the apartment number and zip code.
2. List the full name, address and phone number of your employer(s).
3. Describe and state the location of each piece of real estate in which you own any interest.
4. Give the name, address, phone number, and description of the nature of any business venture in which you own any interest.
5. List the names, addresses, and phone numbers of all persons who owe money to you and specify the amounts owed.
6. List the names and address of all banks and savings institutions where you may have any sums of money deposited and identify the accounts by number.
7. List and give the present location of all items of personal property owned by you that have a value of more than $100.

VERIFICATION

State of _____, County of _____

_____, being first duly sworn on oath, says the foregoing are true and complete answers to the interrogatories propounded by plaintiff to defendant.

Sworn and subscribed before me,
This _____ day of _____, 20__.

_____   _____
Deputy Clerk/Notary Public   Defendant

NOTICE
You are required to provide complete answers to the above stated questions to the plaintiff within 30 days after service of these interrogatories upon you. If you do not answer, or do not answer completely, you may become subject to the sanctions provided by law for Contempt of Court. If you need further instructions or if you need assistance in answering the questions contact the court at once.

134

(Sample Only)

IN THE MAGISTRATE COURT OF _____ COUNTY
STATE OF _____

_____,
Movant,*

vs.   **Civil Action** _____

_____,
Respondent,**

MOTION TO COMPEL DISCOVERY

Comes now movant in the above styled action and files this Motion to compel the respondent to answer interrogatories.

Movant shows the court as follows:

1. That a judgment or fifa was issued by this court.
2. That movant filed Interrogatories upon the respondent by depositing in the United States mail a certified letter, Return receipt requested, with sufficient postage there on. Said return receipt is marked as exhibit "A" and attached hereto; and
3. That there has been an expiration of thirty (30) days since receipt of said interrogatories, and the respondent has failed and refused to answer such questions as propounded.

WHEREFORE, movant moves this court for an Order:

1. Compelling the respondent to show cause why an Oder should not issue compelling respondent to answer said interrogatories; and
2. Compelling the respondent to answer said Interrogatories or in lieu thereof suffer the penalties of contempt and possible incarceration in the common jail of _____ County; and
3. Granting any other relief as justice requires.

_____
Movant

*Movant (one who makes a motion to a court)
**Respondent (a defending party who answers something in a law case)

(Sample Only)

IN THE MAGISTRATE COURT OF _____ COUNTY
STATE OF _____

_____,
   Movant,

vs.   **Civil Action** _____

_____,
   Respondent,

RULE NISI

The within and foregoing Application for Citation for Contempt having been filed in this court, it is hereby set down for a hearing on the _____ day of _____, 20___, at _____ a.m. or p.m.., Courtroom _____, (courthouse address) for the respondent to show cause why an Order for Contempt should not be granted.

This _____ day of _____, 20___.

                                   _____
                                   Deputy Clerk
                                   Magistrate Court

(Sample Only)

IN THE MAGISTRATE COURT OF _____ COUNTY
STATE OF _____

_____,

      Movant,

                        Civil Action _____

vs.

_____,

      Respondent,

APPLICATION FOR CITATION OF CONTEMPT

Comes now the movant above and moves this court to attach the respondent for contempt upon the following grounds:

1. The respondent resides at _____, _____ County, (State) and is subject to the jurisdiction of this court.
2. The respondent on the ____ day of _____, 20___, was served with a copy of an order of this honorable court compelling him to answer within (10) days after receipt thereof, the propounded and interrogatories previously filed upon respondent.
3. That (10) days has elapsed since respondent received a copy of said Order and yet respondent has failed and refused contemptuously to answer said interrogatories without reason.

WHEREFORE, movant moves this court for an Order:

a) Requiring the respondent to show cause why an Order should not issue to incarcerate said respondent for said contempt; and
b) Requiring the respondent answers said interrogatories; and
c) Requiring the respondent to pay prior to his release reasonable attorney fees in connection with the bringing of this Application for Citation of Contempt; and
d) Granting any other relief as justice requires.

_____

         Movant

Figure 14: Satisfaction of Judgment

(Sample Only)

IN THE MAGISTRATE COURT OF _____ COUNTY
STATE OF _____

_____,
           Plaintiff,

                                        Civil Action _____

vs.

_____,
           Defendant,

SATISFACTION OF JUDGMENT

     The debt for which the judgment was rendered has been satisfied between the parties;
     Therefore, the Clerk of Court is hereby authorized and directed to mark the docket "Satisfied of Record".

     This the _____ day of _____, _____.

                                        _____
                                        Plaintiff's signature

This concludes the topic of "Pursuing", and brings to a close my guide to helping you avoid conflicts when purchasing or selling goods and services, starting with properly negotiating a contract, followed by solving disputes prior to a lawsuit by talking to your adversary and, when all else fails, preparing for small claims court and collecting or repaying a debt. It is my hope that you found some benefit from what I've written and can share this newly acquired knowledge with family and friends. Once again, however, I wish to stress that nothing in this book should be taken and/or used as legal advice. To obtain answers to legal questions, it is always best to consult with an attorney.